POSITION TRADING

BUY like a Trader and HOLD like an Investor

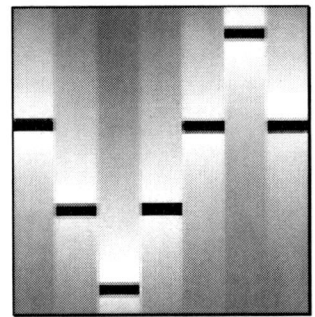

Tony Loton

LOTON *tech*

www.lotontech.com

Copyright © Tony Loton / LOTONtech Limited 2011.

This edition published by LOTONtech Limited (www.lotontech.com).

ISBN-13: 978-0-9559893-3-9

ISBN-10: 0-9559893-3-7

All rights reserved. No part of this publication may be reproduced or distributed in any form or by any means without the prior permission of the author and / or publisher.

The material in this book is provided for educational purposes only. No responsibility for loss occasioned to any person or corporate body acting or refraining to act as a result of reading material in this book can be accepted by the author or publisher.

All trademarks are the property of their respective owners. LOTONtech Limited is not associated with any product or vendor mentioned in this book except where stated.

Unless otherwise stated; any third-party quotes, images and screenshots, or portions thereof, are included under 'fair use' for comment, news reporting, teaching, scholarship, and research.

The majority of the stock and index charts are included courtesy of *Yahoo! Finance UK & Ireland* unless otherwise stated.

Early praise for the first edition of **POSITION TRADING**:
Source: comments from reviewers of the original first edition manuscript.

"I think it is a great book, I certainly will be recommending it."

"I want to try to apply the techniques to my trading and investing."

"It reads well, has an organised structure, and you convey ideas clearly."

"It gets the key principles across without all the padding that you can find in other trading books."

"It is a really good book and I have no hesitation in recommending it to others."

"It reads well and is well organised."

Reader reviews of the first edition of **POSITION TRADING**:
Source: Amazon.co.uk

"This is the first investment strategy book that had me actually wanting to read more the minute I put it down for a break."

"Don't buy a Technical Analysis book and lose all your money in a month, buy this book instead and give yourself a significantly better chance of making money."

Early praise for the second edition of **POSITION TRADING**:
Source: comments from reviewers of the second edition manuscript.

"I still believe this is one of the best systems out there, mainly for its simplicity but also because I just can't see how it could ever lose long term if the trader trades it correctly."

"I challenge you to find any other trading Author or full time Trader who has had the courage and integrity to publicly document all of their trades using the strategy they are promoting."

Contents

About the Author	11
About the Cover Picture and Logo	13
Acknowledgements	13
About the Precursor Books	15
About the Second Edition of POSITION TRADING	17
TALE OF THREE TRADING AUTHORS	17
1 – Introduction to Position Trading	19
RACING POSITIONS	21
POSITION TRADING INSTRUMENTS, MARKETS, AND PLATFORMS	22
THE LONG AND SHORT OF POSITION TRADING	23
ORGANISATION OF CHAPTERS	24
KEEPING IT SIMPLE	25
BIG MONEY, LOW RISK!	26
READY, AIM...	26
2 – On Diversification	29
ARE INDICES DIVERSIFIED?	30
NURTURE AND PRUNE	30
DIVERSIFICATION OVER TIME	31
THE PROBLEM WITH TRADITIONAL DIVERSIFICATION	32

PLANTING THE SEEDS	33
PROTECTION AGAINST PRICE GAPS	34
DIVERSIFICATION BETWEEN PLATFORMS	35
LONG-SHORT DIVERSIFICATION	35
IS DIVERSIFICATION ENOUGH?	36
3 – On Stop Orders	**37**
STOP ORDERS	37
TRAILING STOP ORDERS	39
AUTOMATED STOPS AND MENTAL STOPS	40
STOP DISTANCES	40
STOP ORDERS IN POSITION TRADING	41
THE STOP ORDER DANGER ZONE	46
GUARANTEED STOPS AND MINIMUM STOP DISTANCES	48
4 – On Position Sizing	**51**
DAY TRADER'S APPROACH	51
INVESTOR'S APPROACH	51
POSITION TRADER'S APPROACH	52
POSITION SIZING AND STOP ORDERS	52
POSITION SIZING AND "VALUE AT RISK"	53
POSITION SIZING AND OPTIONS	54

INITIAL AND ONGOING POSITION SIZE	55

5 – On Pyramiding   57

ABOUT "AVERAGING DOWN"	57
PYRAMIDING AND "AVERAGING UP"	58
REAL-LIFE PYRAMIDING EXAMPLE	60
PYRAMIDING AND STOP ORDERS	61
AVERAGING DOWN WITH STOP ORDERS	62
TOP-HEAVY AND BOTTOM-HEAVY PYRAMIDS	63
FUNDING FOR PYRAMIDING	63
WHEN TO PYRAMID	67
REBUILDING A PYRAMID	68
BEWARE OVERWEIGHT PYRAMIDS	68
NON-SPECIFIC PYRAMIDING	69

6 – On Leverage   71

WHAT IS LEVERAGE?	71
LEVERAGE AND MARGIN	72
SPREAD BETTING	73
LEVERAGED OPTIONS	74
WHAT LEVERAGE IS NOT	76
MAKING A LITTLE GO A LONG WAY	76

IS LEVERAGE DANGEROUS?	76

7 – On Stock Picking — 79

ON POSITION ENTRY	79
THE WHAT AND WHEN OF STOCK PICKING	80
THE LIVING WATCH LIST AND THE STOP-OUT LIST	80
BUYING ON SHORT-TERM PRICE ACTION	82
BUYING ON MARKET WEAKNESS	86
BUYING FOR LONG TERM POTENTIAL	87
RISK AND REWARD	88
LOW PRICE MEANS LOW RISK	93
CATCHING A FALLING KNIFE WITH THE SOLD LIST	95
AUTOMATED POSITION ENTRY	99
MARKET TIMING	103
NOT (QUITE) TREND FOLLOWING	103
STOCK PICKING IN A NUTSHELL	105
INCORPORATING YOUR OWN CRITERIA	105

8 – On Dividends — 107

BENEFITS OF DIVIDENDS	107
OFFSETTING ACCOUNT FEES WITH DIVIDENDS	108
DIVIDENDS ON SPREAD BETS	109

Concrete Examples of Offsetting Fees with Dividends	109
Why not look for High Yield?	111

9 – Synthesis — 113

The Seven Pillars of Position Trading	113
Daily Routine	114
When to Sell	118
Not the Buying or Selling, but the Waiting	120
On Drawing Down and Staying Solvent	120
What about Short Position Trading?	122
The Three Phases of Position Trading	126
Effect of Interest Rates	126
What about Other Financial Instruments?	127
Position Trading for Fundamental Investors	128
Defensive Trading	129
Does it Really Work?	130

10 – Proof of the Pudding — 131

From Loser to Winner	131
3000% in Six Months (2009)	132
Trading Trail, January to April 2010	133
Trading Trail, the Great Unravel	137

TRADING TRAIL, THE FIGHT-BACK	141
ON LUCK AND SKILL	142
FUTURE PROOF	143
WILL IT WORK FOR YOU?	144
SCALING UP	146
SO WHAT DOES THIS PROVE?	147
ARE YOU READY TO GIVE UP THE DAY JOB?	147
11 – Automating the Strategy	**149**
WHAT TO AUTOMATE	149
AUTOMATION OPTIONS	150
CONSTRUCTING THE MICROSOFT EXCEL SPREADSHEET	153
ALL DONE FOR YOU	162
NOT ONLY MICROSOFT EXCEL	162
12 – Q & A	**165**
COMMENT ABOUT INITIAL RISKS LIMITED TO 1%	165
COMMENT ABOUT VARIABLE INITIAL RISKS	165
COMMENT ABOUT RISK CALCULATIONS	166
COMMENT ABOUT TECHNICAL VS. FUNDAMENTAL ANALYSIS	166
COMMENTS ABOUT BECOMING PROFITABLE	167
COMMENT ABOUT BUYING FALLERS	168

COMMENT ABOUT RE-BUYING LOWER	168
COMMENTS ABOUT GUARANTEED STOPS AND SLIPPAGE	169
COMMENT ABOUT TRADING THE NEWS	169
COMMENT ABOUT DETERMINING STOP LEVELS	170
COMMENT ABOUT TRADING INDICES	170
COMMENT ABOUT TRADING BREAKOUTS	171
COMMENT ABOUT VOLATILE MARKETS AND RISK CAPITAL	171
COMMENT ABOUT SHARE CONSOLIDATIONS	171
COMMENT ABOUT PYRAMIDING	172
COMMENT ABOUT CONCENTRATION VS. DIVERSIFICATION	172
COMMENT ABOUT WIN / LOSS RATIO	173
COMMENT ABOUT ACCOUNT SIZE	173
COMMENT ABOUT TREND FOLLOWING	174
COMMENT ABOUT STOCK PICKING	174
COMMENT ABOUT RISING (AND FALLING) TIDES	175
COMMENT ABOUT OVERNIGHT FINANCING / ROLLING CHARGES	175
COMMENT ABOUT STOP DISTANCES	175
COMMENT ABOUT PYRAMIDING	176
13 – Visit Me	**177**
Appendix A – Support and Resistance	**179**

SUPPORT	179
RESISTANCE	180
ONE MAN'S SUPPORT IS ANOTHER MAN'S RESISTANCE	181
Appendix B – Definitions of "Position Trading"	**183**
Also by Tony Loton	**185**
PUBLISHED BY HARRIMAN HOUSE	185
PUBLISHED BY LOTON*TECH* LIMITED	186
Table of Figures	**187**
Index	**191**

About the Author

Tony Loton trades a range of financial instruments including equities, exchange traded funds, covered warrants, and spread bets on his own account. He would describe himself as a graduate of the Investment School of Hard Knocks.

Tony has written regularly for the Barclays Stockbrokers "Smart Investor" magazine and its associated email program, and has also written for the Motley Fool (UK) web site.

He has previously written and published financial titles including "DON'T LOSE MONEY! (in the Stock Markets)", "Financial Trading Patterns", and "Stock Fundamentals On Trial : Do Dividend Yield, P/E and PEG Really Work?"

In October 2008, Tony was featured as a day trader in the Money section of the UK's Sunday Times, and in 2009 he was commissioned by Harriman House publishers to write a book on the subject of "Stop Orders".

Tony published the Trading Trail year-long blog in 2010, which documented a 'live' public run of the Position Trading strategy with associated commentary.

You can find out more about Tony Loton's trading and investment books, and access his latest blog, at:

www.lotontech.com/positiontrading

Please note that Tony Loton is not authorised to give financial or tax advice, and in this book he merely documents and demonstrates the trading-cum-investment approach that has worked for him.

About the Cover Picture and Logo

Besides looking more visually appealing than the styling of the first edition book cover, the new cover picture and chapter-head logo provides a visual representation of some of the key aspects of the Position Trading approach.

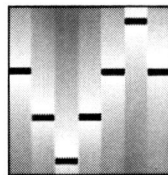

The red and blue gradients represent profit and loss, or price increases and decreases, and the graphic equaliser-style slide indicators represent separate competing stock 'positions' at various profit levels.

Acknowledgements

I'd like to thank all those who agreed to review the original manuscript of this book, for no more reward than an acknowledgement here and a free copy of the book.

Thanks especially to those followers of my Trading Trail blog who provided valuable feedback on the first and second edition manuscripts. They were Greg Maddocks, H. A. Booth, Pierre Fachon, Adrian Bryant, George Ferris and Glynn Clarkson.

About the Precursor Books

Some of you reading this will be aware that I have previously written other trading and investment books, and you might be wondering how those previous works – along with this work – fit in to the overall picture. You may even have detected some apparent inconsistencies in my approach, which is a necessary consequence of the changing market conditions and my own evolution as a trader and investor.

Having previously lost a not-insignificant amount of money at the 'Investment School of Hard Knocks' while teaching myself to trade, I emphasised the absolute importance of protecting against downside risk (rather than buying and blindly holding) in my book "DON'T LOSE MONEY! (in the Stock Markets)". I also hinted at the futility of making individual stock selections based entirely on *fundamental analysis*; and instead suggested a technical – possibly mechanical – approach to trading stock indices.

In my book "Financial Trading Patterns" I took the mechanisation idea further by formalising the use of stop orders and limit orders in combination to achieve specific trading objectives such as buy low, sell high and buy high, sell higher. As a counter-balance to the key messages, I showed that a purely mechanical trading system based on predetermined one-size-fits-all parameters (such as one-size-fits-all stop distances) would not be effective under all market conditions.

I returned to the idea of stock fundamentals, and in particular the danger of simplistic fundamental analysis, in my book "Stock Fundamentals On Trial: Do Dividend Yield, P/E and PEG Really Work?" In this book I demonstrated to my own satisfaction that screening stocks simply for favourable fundamental ratios, and then holding those stocks indefinitely regardless of subsequent price action, was potentially a recipe for disaster.

In my first book for Harriman House publishers, "Stop Orders", I described what I deem to be the most important weapon in the trader's armoury: the stop order. In addition to presenting the theory and practice of stop orders, I sowed the seeds for the Trading Trail blog – and subsequently the book you are reading now – by conducting a limited public experiment in which I grew an initial minimal stake of just under £300 to more than £9000 in only six months: using a combination of stop orders, position sizing, pyramiding, and leverage.

Taken altogether, the set of precursor books was leading up to something:

This Book on Position Trading.

About the Second Edition of POSITION TRADING

I published the first edition of this book shortly after embarking on my Trading Trail 2010 daily blog in which I published my real 'position' trades and my rationales for making those trades. I revised and updated the book for the second edition towards the end of the Trading Trail year-long run having discovered how difficult it is to trade *in public view*.

To illustrate how difficult it is, consider my...

Tale of Three Trading Authors

Trading Author #1 - "Theory Henri"

He writes for a well-known investment web site, telling readers 'in theory' how stop orders, leverage, and any form of 'timing' are dangerous, and how the Long Term Buy and Hold (LTBH) approach is the only approach that works. Despite his own unpublished and not-admitted poor results over the past decade, he knows it works because he read in a book that it worked for some people a few decades ago. He can never be proved wrong.

Trading Author #2 - "Simon Survivorship"

He runs ten different trading accounts in private, using ten different strategies. When he decides that one of them has come good (and one of them is bound to come good over some period from three months to ten years) he publishes his guaranteed make-a-million strategy, conveniently forgetting that nine of the strategies didn't work and that the one that did work may have done so as a result of pure chance.

Tony Loton

Trading Author #3 - "Crazy Tony"

He fixes *in advance* his trading strategy (Position Trading), his timescale (one calendar year), his trading funds (£1000), and his trading platform (initially the 'Shorts and Longs' spread betting platform). He has no classical theory to hide behind, no benefit of hindsight or survivorship bias, and is further constrained by committing to educate (even if by failing) and entertain as he goes.

As the situation evolves, should he walk away when he 'cashes out' at exactly the right time for a 60% profit within just three months -- thus reneging on the commitment to blog for a year?

Should he stick doggedly with the original platform, and not show how a different platform without guaranteed stops but with lower rolling charges can perform better or (it seems) worse?

Should he scale back his ambitions by sticking exactly to the original trading budget, which turned out to be enough to merely 'stay solvent' but not to realise the full potential of the strategy?

Those questions are rhetorical, but they serve to illustrate the difficulty in implementing my plan to educate and amuse while making money over a fixed timescale with a fixed amount of money.

On the other hand, the Trading Trail – which wasn't a complete disaster, by the way – served its purpose as a rich source of additional material, lessons learned, and readers' comments for this second edition of...

POSITION TRADING

BUY like a Trader and HOLD like an Investor

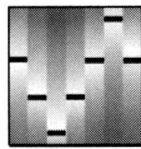

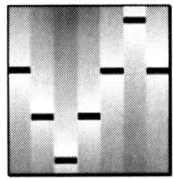

1 – Introduction to Position Trading

Over a number of years I tried my hand at almost every trading and investment style: short-term day trading, long-term buy and hold, index trading, equity trading, mutual fund investment, options trading, market timing, swing trading, fundamental investing, and mechanical trading – not to mention entrusting my money to a *professional* money manager.

Some trading styles worked a little, some worked occasionally, and some did not work at all (to put it mildly). Only one trading style has worked *for me* consistently and profitably, and that is *position trading*. So while occasionally I do still engage in other trading and investment styles; I would regard myself these days as primarily a *position trader*.

If you're unfamiliar with this term, you can think of me as a trader-investor. If a trade turns against me, I will sell out for a small loss – or better still, at a profit – even if this means holding a position for less than a day. On the other hand I will hold on to a position potentially forever, as long as the price keeps rising or at least not falling while I collect some dividends along the way.

Thus my preferred period to hold a stock or other financial instrument is *forever* – just like Warren Buffett – but this is only my *preferred* holding period rather than an obligation. I'm not talking about Long Term Buy and Hold (LTBH) and certainly not Long Term Buy and Forget (LTBF).

The idea of a short-term trade becoming a long-term investment may be familiar to you. I'm sure you have heard the following phrase:

"A long term investment is a short term trade gone *bad*."

It refers to the tendency for novice traders to hold on to a failing trade for as long as possible until it recovers – if at all.

I like to turn that phrase entirely on its head, like this:

"A long term investment is a short term trade gone *well*."

It means that I will open a position with the intention of *cutting my loss* quickly if the trade turns against me, rather like a day trader would do. But I will hold onto a position that performs well, thus *letting my profit run* for as long as I can, rather like an investor would do.

Unlike day trading, swing trading, and other short-to-medium-term trading approaches, my position trading approach might present a viable alternative for those of you who consider yourselves to be 'investors'.

In this book I offer my interpretation of *position trading*, and the way that I practice it. Some traders and authors may define position trading as holding a position with a timeframe of weeks or months, and definitely not as short as days, but I specify no fixed timescale in advance. Some people liken position trading to buy-and-hold, but I do not. Some people regard position trading as synonymous with *trend following*, and that may be closer to what I do.

"I will hold a position for as long as possible – but no longer!"

(See *Appendix B – Definitions of "Position Trading"* for alternative definitions of the term position trading.)

By not drawing on too many external sources, I hope to present this trading style in a way that may not be totally familiar to you; in a way that does not make you think that you've heard it all before. In fact you may not have heard it all before, because whereas books and articles have been published on the key concepts of *stop orders*, *position sizing*, *leverage* and *pyramiding*, no book to my knowledge has yet (at the time of the first edition) brought together these techniques under the title *Position Trading*.

Although this book is designed to be as original as possible, it doesn't mean that I'm the first person to adopt this trading style or that it is unproven. Position trading is a recognized trading strategy, and I have proven to my own satisfaction that it works – using my own money. And there is no better proof than putting your own money where your mouth is.

While there are currently no books exclusively on the subject of Position Trading – well, none listed on Amazon.com with this title at the time of writing the first edition – there is of course *some* literature on the subject. If and when I draw on it in this book, I'll tell you.

Racing Positions

I understand that *position trading* is so named because it involves establishing and holding a *position* in a stock or commodity. But I have an alternative interpretation of the term.

I regard my numerous simultaneous stock positions rather like motor cars in a long distance endurance race, each jostling for *position*. But this is a race with a difference, because in this race:

- I can place bets on any or all of the racers.
- I can alter those bets at any time during the race, increasing my stakes on those racers who look more likely to win.

- I can take back some, or all, of my initial stake on any racer that falls behind.

But it's not just about running a number of *positions*. It's also about being *correctly positioned* for the onset of a major trend. As a 'long' trader I would ideally like to be fully invested (have no free cash) at exactly the bottom of a bear market and to be not invested at all (or be 'short') at the top; which is not as easy as it sounds.

Position Trading Instruments, Markets, and Platforms

In principle it is possible to position-trade a wide range of financial instruments in a range of markets via a variety of platforms, but there are subtleties that make some choices better than others:

Position trading equities (stocks), and indices in the form of Exchange Traded Funds (ETFs) would be preferable to position trading currencies or commodities, because equities and indices pay dividends. But this doesn't rule out currencies and commodities absolutely, and you might also consider position trading bonds.

Position trading using spread bets (or spread trades as they are sometimes called) offers some advantages over trading via a regular stockbroker account because spread betting is tax-free (in the UK at least), there are no stockbroker commissions to pay, and you can take advantage of leverage by depositing only an initial 'margin' amount. But the investment-like nature of position trading does lend itself to operation through regular stockbroker accounts – including tax-efficient retirement accounts – in a way that rapid day trading and swing trading do not. Indeed, the longer a position is held, the more attractive the one-off transaction charge levied by a regular stockbroker becomes compared with the ongoing *rolling charges* levied by the spread betting firms.

POSITION TRADING

My interpretation of position trading assumes no fixed timescale at the outset, which to some extent rules out covered warrants and other fixed-term options that require your trade to 'come good' by a certain date. It is not impossible to position trade leveraged options, but my recommendation would be to choose those that have very far-into-the-future expiry dates.

My position trading approach relies on the use of stop orders to limit losses and secure accrued profits, and you may find that your stockbroker does not allow automated stop orders on some financial instruments such as options and mutual funds. This need not rule out the use of stop orders as long as you are disciplined enough to record, and then ruthlessly apply, your own *mental stop orders*.

Since position trades start of as short-term trades that subsequently become long-term investments, in the early stages of a trade it may be useful to have access to traders' data: real-time charts and Level 2 data. Fear not if your stockbroker does not provide Level 2 data, and if you only have access to charts that are delayed by 15 minutes; it just means that you will have to tweak the approach to rely more on position sizing than tight initial stop orders.

The Long and Short of Position Trading

Since traders are known to trade both long (bet on rising prices) and short (bet on falling prices) you might be wondering if position trading can be practiced on the short side. In theory the answer is yes, but you might smell a rat:

I told you that a position trader will let a short term trade become a long term investment, and it may sound somewhat illogical to have a long term investment on the short side. Indeed, whereas a long trade has potentially unlimited upside potential and strictly limited downside potential (because a price cannot fall below zero), a short trade has strictly limited upside potential (because, once again, the price can only fall as far a zero). Since a price cannot fall forever, one cannot hold a short trade indefinitely.

You might smell another rat:

I told you that I might hope to collect dividends on a position trade, and you will no doubt have figured out that collecting dividends is not possible on a short trade. In fact, you may well have to pay dividends on a short trade in a spread betting account!

So with those two provisos – that your profit potential is limited, and you cannot collect dividends along the way – it is still possible to position trade a short position. But in this book I'll assume you (and me) to be predominantly trading long.

Organisation of Chapters

Many people regard trading and investment as being all about clever stock picking, and many of you reading this book will be eager to get to the chapter that tells you which stocks to buy. You'll have to wait, I'm afraid, because I have relegated this information to *Chapter 7 – On Stock Picking*.

I firmly believe that successful position trading is more about effective money management using diversification, stop orders, position sizing, and leverage, than it is about picking the right stocks. Choosing the right investments at the right time will help you to maximize your returns in the long run, but only sound money management will help you to stay in the game long enough to realize those returns. So I tackle these topics first in *Chapters 2 through 6*.

While I'm not a high yield investor who seeks out those stocks with the highest dividend yield (which I think is a somewhat dubious approach in any case), in *Chapter 8 – On Dividends* I explain why I prefer to position-trade dividend-paying stocks rather than commodities, currencies, or other financial instruments.

Having covered the underlying principles of the approach: the seven pillars of position trading; in *Chapter 9 – Synthesis* I present my synthesis of the separate techniques.

You will of course be keen to see some evidence that this approach really does work, and in *Chapter 10 – Proof of the Pudding* I present my own real-life results. One of my motivations in writing this book was to document the trading approach that allowed me to make a 3000%+ return in the middle six months of 2009, and then more than 50% return in the first quarter of 2010. But it wasn't all plain sailing, as you will see!

In *Chapter 11 – Automating the Strategy*, which is a new chapter in this edition of the book, I discuss the 'Position Trading Cockpit' Excel spreadsheet that I devised to help automate some aspects of the strategy.

In *Chapter 12 – Q & A* I recall some of the comments posted by readers in the course of my Trading Trail 2010 blog, and I give my answers.

Keeping it Simple

Trading and investment is often portrayed as more complicated than it needs to be; whereas my *position trading* approach is focused on *keeping it simple*.

You won't find me identifying any *dojis, hanging men, cups-with-handles,* or any other exotic *technical analysis* patterns in this book – with the possible exceptions of *price support / resistance levels* (see *Appendix A – Support and Resistance*) and *price gaps / spikes*. You won't find any mention of *P/E, PEG, Dividend Yield,* or any other fundamental ratio except in passing.

It's all about good old fashioned money management, which in summary means:

- Buying low with a small initial stake.

- Adding more as the price goes up.

- Always protecting the downside using stop orders.

Of course it's a little more complicated than that in practice, but not as complicated as many books and web resources will have you think.

Big Money, Low Risk!

As you work through the chapters that follow, keep in mind the fact that my *position trading* approach is designed to make Big Money (by *pyramiding*, through *leverage*, and with a little clever *stock picking*) with Low Risk (thanks to *stop orders, position sizing,* and *diversification*).

Before you go throwing you life savings into this strategy, I should clarify what I mean by low risk. This is not a wealth preservation strategy, so if you've already made a lot of money elsewhere you should probably keep it safe under the mattress. If you have £1000 to spare – and I mean 'to spare' – and you manage to increase it by 3000% (see *Chapter 10 – Proof of the Pudding*) then the £500 (i.e. a massive 50%) you lost en route would seem like a small risk as a proportion of your final cash pile of £30,000!

Ready, Aim...

Are you ready? Shall we aim together for a big profit this year?

If you answered 'yes', consider this:

It always amuses me when I read about investment funds or fund managers that aim to achieve a specific return per annum, let's say

10%. If we are able to aim with any degree of accuracy, why not aim for 100% or 1000% or even 3000%? If you aim for a 10% return per annum, what do you do when you achieve it? Pack up for the year, like I should have done with the 60% return that I banked in the first quarter of 2010?

Aiming to lose no more than 10% by placing stop orders on a diverse group of equities in your regular brokerage account, or by staking only £1,000 of your £10,000 cash pile in your spread betting account, is a much better aim in my opinion. Look after the downside and let the upside look after itself.

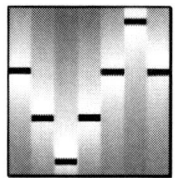

2 – On Diversification

Some people say that we should spread our eggs between several baskets. With many baskets scattered all throughout the forest, Mr. Fox won't find all of them. But he will find some.

Some people (including Warren Buffett) say that we should put all our eggs in one basket – and watch it carefully. Standing over our one basket with a big gun ensures that all our eggs are safe from Mr. Fox, providing we don't fall asleep.

There is a third way, which is to put our eggs in several baskets – and watch them all. With several baskets scattered throughout the forest, each with its own armed guard, we can truly out-fox Mr. Fox.

This principle underlies my position trading philosophy.

The eggs I'm talking about are my hard-earned pounds, or dollars, or Euros; and the baskets I'm talking about are my individual equity positions.

As you will see in *Chapter 3 – On Stop Orders*, each equity position (or basket) has its own armed guard in the form of a *stop order*. And as you will see in *Chapter 5 – On Pyramiding*, each equity position (or basket) attracts more money (or eggs) the longer it remains undiscovered by Mr. Fox; or in the context of the stock markets – Mr. Bear.

Are Indices Diversified?

I have been known to trade stock indices such as the FTSE 100 (UK), Dow Jones 30 (USA), or DAX (Germany), but not for the purposes of diversification.

Contrary to popular belief, stock indices do not – in my opinion – provide the right kind of diversification because you have to buy or sell the index as a whole. You have no way of locking in the gains on the individual constituents; so for all intents and purposes all of your eggs are in *one basket*. It's just that the basket contains a variety of eggs: some that Mr. Fox (or Mr. Bear) will take a liking to and some that he won't. There are far too many for him to wolf down (another animal, I know) all at once, so – on the plus side – at least you're protected from a total wipe-out.

Since you have no control over the individual constituents, the only way to make money on indices, over and above the much-touted long-term index returns, is by employing the kind of market timing that I described in my earlier book "DON'T LOSE MONEY! (in the Stock Markets)". In other words: you can make money on stock indices only by *watching them carefully* and not by simply holding them.

For completeness I should say that there is another problem associated with relying on major indices for diversification: the fact that popular capitalisation-weighted indices such as the FTSE 100 can easily become dominated by just a few companies from a limited number of sectors.

Nurture and Prune

I'm no gardener, but it seems logical to me that the best way to manage a garden is to plant lots of different seeds, at different times throughout the Spring; to nurture those that thrive, by feeding and watering them; and to cut back, dig up, or prune the ones that are clearly not going to make it through the winter – and which will in the meantime take some of the sustenance away from the fittest flowers.

I'm not alone in this view. In the context of nature, Charles Darwin introduced the idea of *survival of the fittest*; and in the context of investment many successful investors have advised that we should *water the flowers* by introducing more funds into the winners, and *cut the weeds* by ditching the losers. Yet many novices *cut the flowers* by cashing out at the first sign of profit, and water the weeds by 'averaging down' on the losers.

We'll water the flowers by *pyramiding* additional money into winning positions (*Chapter 5 – On Pyramiding*) and we'll cut the weeds with the help of *stop orders* (*Chapter 3 – On Stop Orders*).

It's what you might call a "devil take the hindmost" strategy.

Diversification over Time

For this nurture-and-prune approach to work, we need a large number of seedlings from which to choose, which means that we need to plant lots of seeds – but not necessarily all at the same time. Different seeds are better planted at different times of the year, and it's the same with stock purchases. In my *position trading* approach we'll establish each new equity position when it makes sense to do so; when the price is attractive and when the upside potential is greater than the downside risk.

In the context of asset classes rather than individual equities, consider this:

If you think that Gold and the FTSE 100 index are negatively correlated (i.e. one goes up when the other goes down) then it obviously makes sense to invest half of your money in Gold at the bottom of the Gold cycle (which is the top of the FTSE 100 cycle) and then invest the other half of your money in the FTSE 100 index at the bottom of the FTSE 100 cycle (which is the top of the Gold cycle). Henceforth: as one falls, the other rises exactly to compensate so that your money is always safe, but you locked in some profit by establishing each position at the bottom of its respective cycle.

Don't take this too literally! I'm not stating here that Gold and the FTSE 100 index are perfectly negatively correlated. It's just a hypothetical example.

If you now expand your thinking from these two asset classes, to the hundreds of individual equities, you will start to see why *diversification over time* may be a useful tool in our armoury.

The Problem with Traditional Diversification

The problem with diversification as traditionally taught is that it encourages diversification *all at once* rather than *over time*. This is encouraged by money managers, who for obvious reasons want to get their hands on your funds all at once. But it is also encouraged by the investing public who tend to seek out those very same money managers when they have a lot of money to invest *all at once* (e.g. in the form of an unexpected inheritance) rather than because they have judged it to be the right time to invest.

To be fair, some money managers also encourage drip-feeding of your funds into their products. They'll tell you it's because pound-cost-averaging (or dollar-cost-averaging) works, and so it might, but I rather suspect they recommend this to those people who simply don't have a lump sum to invest all at once.

So the money manager gets his hands on your lump sum and invests it in a diversified S&P 500 index fund. If the constituent stocks that fall within the index are offset exactly by those that rise – as you would expect in a perfectly diversified portfolio – you'll just about break even over time, minus the money manager's fees. You might even benefit *eventually* from the much-publicized long-run average market return (let's say 7%) as long as you don't cash-in during one of the inevitable bear markets – like the one from 2000 to 2003, or the one from 2007 to 2009 – in which the whole diversified S&P 500 index fell significantly.

In this scenario wouldn't it have been better to keep some powder dry (i.e. money available) to as to benefit from the 'on sale' stock prices at the market bottoms, rather than having committed it all at once? Even better: what if you could have held on to the S&P stocks that didn't fall, while ditching the potential losers at the first sign of trouble? Rather than having to keep, or ditch, the whole basket.

Planting the Seeds

So we're going to plant a large number of seeds, over time, from which we can nurture the winners and prune the losers. But which seeds should we plant, and when should we plant them?

This subject will be covered in *Chapter 7 – On Stock Picking*.

I relegate this topic to such a late chapter because I regard *picking the right stocks* as less important than *managing our stock positions* using a combination of *stop orders, position sizing, leverage,* and *pyramiding*. We should not look for candidate stocks until we have a good idea about what we'll do with them once we've bought them.

Protection against Price Gaps

One of the banes of the stock trader is the price gap; when a stock price falls from one price to another apparently instantaneously without any opportunity to trade at prices within the gap. You may have to close a position at a (much) lower price than you would like, and with a stop order in place you may well be sold out automatically at the lower price.

There is little or nothing you can do about this phenomenon apart from utilising guaranteed stop orders (see *Chapter 3 – On Stop Orders*), but by diversifying across a number of positions you limit the effect that any one price gap can have on your whole portfolio.

As a concrete example, take a look at *Figure 1 Desire Petroleum Price Gap*. Notice how the share price halved from 100p to 50p in late April, with little or no opportunity to trade at prices in between. If all your money was invested in Desire Petroleum, you would have lost half of it in an instant! By diversifying your trading or investment funds across ten separate stocks, your portfolio would have taken only a 5% hit.

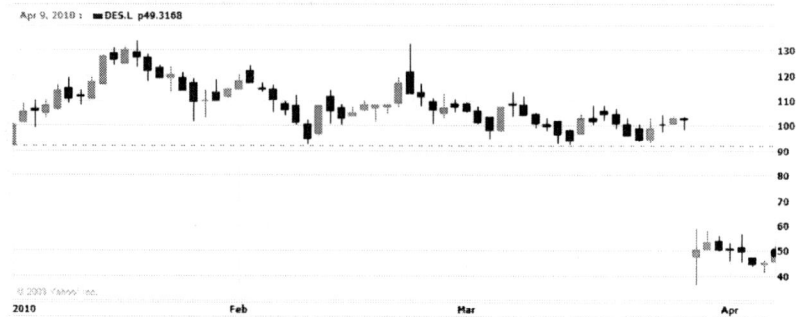

Figure 1 Desire Petroleum Price Gap

One trader's loss is another trader's opportunity, and you will see in *Chapter 7 – On Stock Picking* how you may even be able to benefit from such price gaps.

Diversification between Platforms

Different brokers and spread betting firms treat price gaps differently, and not always consistently. By holding the same position with more than one broker, you may find that you get 'stopped out' (see *Chapter 3 – On Stop Orders*) on one trading platform but not on another. For this reason I sometimes diversify *across platforms*, for example by placing two £1-per-point spread bets on the same stock with different spread betting firms rather than placing a single £2-per-point spread bet with a single firm.

More generally, you will find that your brokers' web sites – and indeed their phone lines – can be 'down' due to technical difficulties; usually when you really need to place or maintain a trade. By trading on more than one platform, you can reduce the chances of having your trading hands temporarily tied.

Do note, however, that trading on more than one platform can be very labour-intensive. And on platforms that charge a per-transaction trading fee, spreading your investment across accounts can be more costly than concentrating on one platform.

Long-Short Diversification

Readers of the first edition of this book pointed out that in addition to diversifying across assets, over time, and between platforms, I could diversify even more by trading in both directions: long and short. While not wishing to alienate those readers who have come from a traditional long-only investment background, I'll acknowledge that this is a perfectly valid point.

Is Diversification Enough?

Some investment advisors regard diversification alone as sufficient protection for your portfolio: you can simply establish (i.e. purchase) a diversified portfolio and forget about it on the assumption that any losing stocks will always be offset by your winning stocks. Not only is this a recipe for mediocre gains, or no gains at all, it is also based on a false assumption. Try telling investors who were caught up in the 1929 Wall Street Crash, the turn-of-the-millennium dot-com crash, or the recent financial crisis, that their *entire portfolio* is unlikely to fall.

Ah, but you should diversify even more widely across markets at home and abroad, they say. Well, guess what? The Dow Jones (USA), FTSE (UK), DAX (Germany), and Nikkei (Japan) indices have a tendency to all rise and fall at the same time.

To be fair, it may be more effective to include non-developed emerging markets and other asset classes (gold, property etc.) in a fully diversified portfolio; but this still does not overcome the fact that diversification's greatest strength – the fact that as something rises, something else falls to compensate – is also its recipe for mediocre gains.

In a nutshell: diversification is *necessary* for investment success, but not *sufficient*.

We must also master the essential money management techniques, beginning with stop orders.

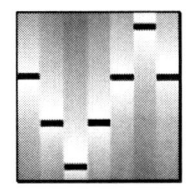

3 – On Stop Orders

In this chapter it is not my intention to replicate the whole of the book that I wrote specifically on the subject of stop orders. I will tell you what you need to know, and no more, about stop orders in the context of my position trading approach. Whether this saves you from having to buy the other book, or inspires you to do so for a deeper understanding, is up to you.

You can find out more about my "Stop Orders" book by turning to the 'Also by Tony Loton' section on page 185 of this book.

Stop Orders

A stop order, more commonly known as a stop-loss order, is a standing order that you place with a stockbroker to close an open *long* position when the price falls to a certain level. You can think of a stop-loss order as a safety net – rather like a trapeze artist's safety net – that stops you falling too far. You decide how much pain you can stand in terms of money lost, and you use the stop order to cap your pain at that level.

Figure 2 Stop Order to "Stop a Loss" shows stylistically how a stop order may be used to *stop a loss*. The stop order is placed at the time that the position is opened, in order to close the position if the price falls too far below the buy-in price; thereby limiting the loss to an acceptable level.

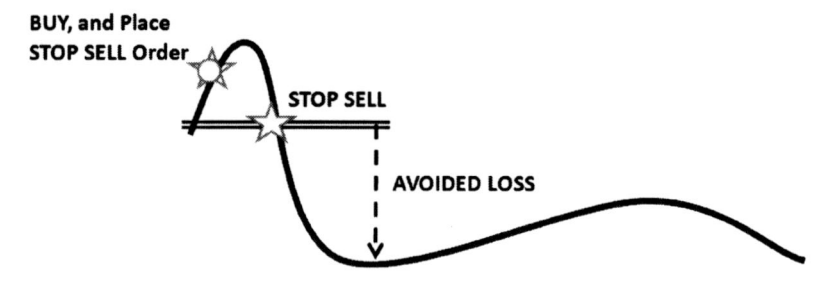

Figure 2 Stop Order to "Stop a Loss"

In the stylistic figures a circle indicates the point at which you place an order and a star indicates the point at which you actually enter or exit a position either manually or as a result of your order executing.

Position traders aim not only to cut their losses, but also to run their profits. A stop order clearly helps you to cut your losses on trades that go the wrong way, but it can also help you to run your profits without having to crystallize those profits prematurely by selling out too soon.

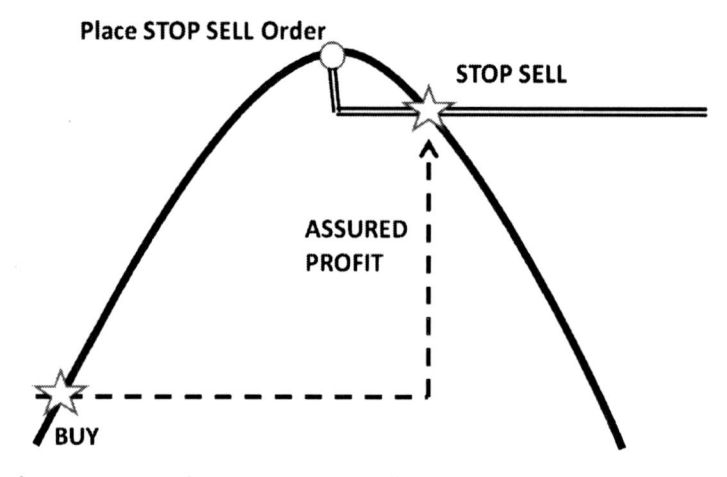

Figure 3 Stop Order to "Secure a Profit" shows stylistically how a stop order may be applied to a profitable position, in order to secure an accrued profit but not crystallize that profit unless it starts to slip away because the price falls.

Figure 3 Stop Order to "Secure a Profit"

This idea of using a stop order to first limit a loss, and then secure a profit, leads us on to the idea of trailing stop orders.

Trailing Stop Orders

A trailing stop order is an order that is adjusted upwards as the price of your holding increases, so as to crystallize an ever smaller loss or ever greater profit when the price trend reverses – but not *until* the price trend reverses.

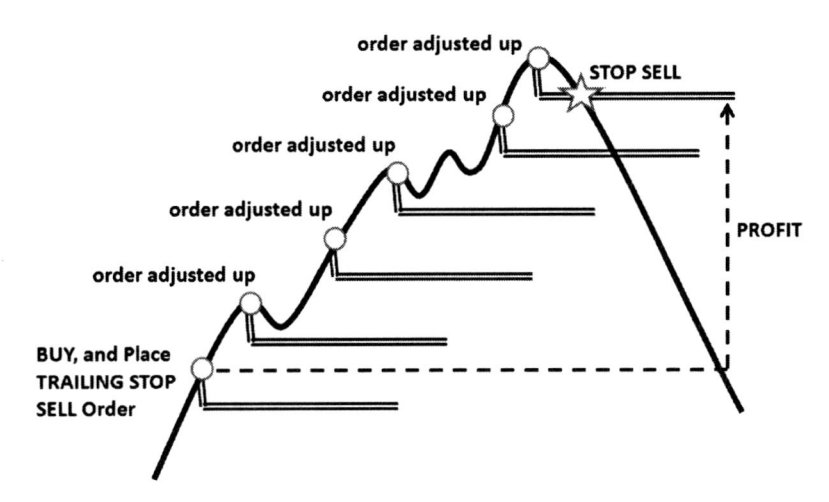

Figure 4 Trailing Stop Order shows stylistically how a trailing stop order can be used to *lock-in* an increasing amount of profit without crystallizing that profit prematurely.

Figure 4 Trailing Stop Order

Some stockbrokers and spread betting providers will let you place an automated trailing stop order on some financial instruments; but not all brokers, and not on all financial instruments. Where a broker does not provide automated trailing stops, you can simply trail them yourself by adjusting the stop-out price of your non-trailing stop order.

Automated Stops and Mental Stops

Many stockbrokers and spread betting providers allow you to place an automated stop order with them, simply by specifying the particular security (e.g. the stock or index) and the level at which to stop out. This feature is not universal, and some financial instruments may not permit the application of automated stop orders: *mutual funds* and *options*, for example. In these cases it is still possible to utilise the stop order concept, by thinking up and writing down your chosen stop level in the form of a 'mental stop'. When the price hits that level, you sell out manually – no questions asked.

Some stockbrokers and spread betting providers will allow you to place automated stop orders, but not automated trailing stop orders. In this case you can use automated stop orders, but you must trail them manually – which, as you will see, is no bad thing.

Stop Distances

The most often asked, and least well answered, question about stop orders is where to place them. Setting your stop level or stop distance (for a trailing stop order) too close to the market price will cause you to be stopped-out prematurely, and frequently, albeit for a small loss. Setting your stop level or stop distance too far below the market price will protect you from frequent stop-outs and associated whipsaw losses, but will crystallize a bigger loss or smaller profit if and when you do get stopped out.

There are several ways to decide on a stop distance including:

- As an arbitrary percentage of the buy-in price. For example: you will sell if the price falls by 10% from any peak. Keep in mind the fact that by the time the price doubles (lucky you!), your position will stop out on a fall of only 5% if you had specified a fixed trailing stop distance as a number of pence or points.

- As a function of historic volatility, using a Beta Adjusted Trailing Stop (BATS) or an Average True Range (ATR) calculation.

- By observing recent support levels, below which the price is unlikely to fall.

If you don't know what a 'support level' is, take a look at Appendix A – Support and Resistance... and then come back here.

Stop Orders in Position Trading

Now, as promised, I'll tell you about how I use stop orders in my position trading strategy.

Buy like a Day Trader

Although I'm happy to hold a position potentially forever, just like Warren Buffett, I do find it disheartening to see that one of my positions has fallen in value as soon as – or soon after – my position has been established. And so will you.

I believe that my first loss (if I take it) will be my smallest, and so I'm not prepared to sit and watch a share price keep falling in the hope that it will recover eventually.

"He who trades, and runs away, lives to trade another day"

My approach is therefore to buy like a *day trader*, in the hope of some immediate profit and the expectation that I will exit the position quickly if such profit fails to materialize. Thus my initial stop orders are usually very tight, but respectful of any recent price support levels.

There are two main exceptions to this rule:

- When the price is so low that it can't fall much further; and where a fall to zero would not wipe me out. For example: on 26 March 2010 I established a £1-per-point spread bet position in Plus Market Group at a price of 3.01p, so I stood to lose a maximum of only £3 even without a stop order.

- Where the trading vehicle imposes a fixed fee on each transaction.

The second point deserves some further explanation:

My preferred trading vehicle is *spread betting*, where the broker's fee is implicit in the bid-ask spread. When trading via a regular brokerage account or on a Contracts for Difference (CFD) platform you will be charged a transaction fee in addition to the albeit-smaller bid-ask spread. A tight stop order that limits your initial loss to only £10 may be counter-productive if it cost you £20 in transaction fees to establish the position in the first place, £20 to stop out, and then a further £20 if you ever decide to re-enter the position.

Where a fixed transaction charge is levied, it would be wise to apply a *wider stop order* in order to reduce the probability of being stopped out unnecessarily.

Notwithstanding the point I've just made, an example tight stop order on my ideal spread betting platform might be as follows.

On 1 March 2010 I established a new £1-per-point spread bet position on Prudential after the price had spiked up, and then down, on news of the company's intention to purchase the Asian business of troubled

POSITION TRADING

US insurer AIG. As you might just about be able to make out in *Figure 5 Prudential 1 March 2010 (tight stop)*, the price bottomed out at around 510p. I would place my initial stop order below this price, but not too far below; perhaps at a price of 495p thereby limiting my initial risk on my £1-per-point bet to: 520 (my purchase price) *minus* 495 (my stop level) = £25 *plus* the bid/ask spread.

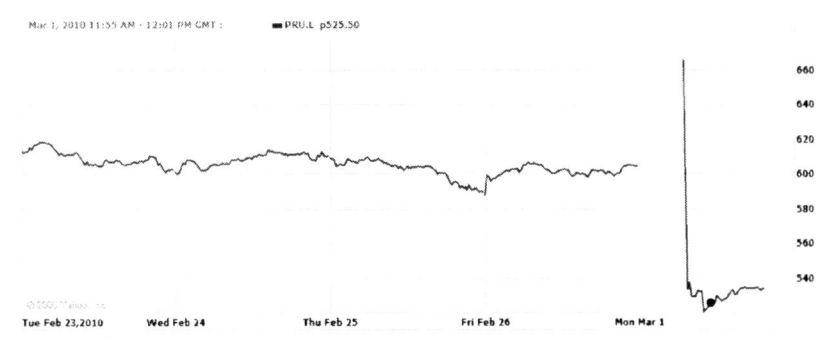

Figure 5 Prudential 1 March 2010 (tight stop)

Bearing in mind what I said about CFD and regular brokerage trades, on an equivalent £1-per-point CFD trade my risk could be as much as: 520 (my purchase price) *minus* 495 (my stop level) = £25 *plus* £20 (transaction fee on the purchase) *plus* £20 (transaction fee on the sale) = £65 *plus* the bid/ask spread. Although the bid/ask spread on the CFD platform is theoretically smaller than on the spread betting platform, this will make little or no difference to the overall loss if we get stopped out.

The situation may be almost as bad when making an investment in a regular brokerage account. With a £500 investment (to give the same profit-per-percent-rise as the £1-per-point spread bet on this stock) my initial risk could be: 495 (my stop level) *divided* by 525 (my purchase price) = 5.7% loss (or £28.50) *plus* £12.50 (transaction fee) to establish the position *plus* £12.50 to close the position = £53.50 *plus* the bid/ask spread. And I've not even accounted for the additional stamp duty that must be paid (in the UK at least) at the time of the purchase.

All is not lost for those who are unable or unwilling to place spread bets, but you must do one of the following things:

- Apply a wider stop (i.e. at a lower price) so that it is less likely to be hit, and so that the fixed transaction charges account for a smaller proportion of the overall monetary risk.

- Trade bigger, e.g. make a £5000 investment or place £10-per-point CFD stake, so that the fixed transaction charges account for a smaller proportion of the overall stake.

Hold like an Investor

Regardless of how tight or how wide I place my initial stop order, my aim is to let the stop distance grow to about 15%-to-20% below the prevailing market price before trailing it upwards in line with the rising price.

This is because I really don't want to get stopped out at all once my position is in profit. I'd like to hold my stock positions forever, and – just like an investor – bank the dividends along the way *as long as the price keeps rising*.

The purpose of my trailing stop order is therefore to *lock-in an increasing amount of profit,* rather than to *stop a loss;* and all the while I'm trying hard to *not get stopped out*.

Here follows an example of how I might set a tight stop order initially, and then begin to trail it (manually) when the time is right.

Rank Group Trailing Stop Example

Figure 6 Rank Group Initial Stop and Trailing Stop provides a concrete example in the context of my Rank Group position. I bought at a price of 88.20 on 5 February 2010. My initial stop level was at 85p, and I kept to this stop level while the price increased from 15 February onwards; until I could adjust the stop order upwards to a level no closer than 15% below the prevailing market price. With the price at about 112 at the end of the chart, I could – on the first day of March – safely trail my stop order up to the 94p level.

At this point I had locked-in a guaranteed profit of 6 points, which would amount to £60 GBP profit on a £10-per-point spread bet or £68 (6.8%) on a £1000 traditional investment.

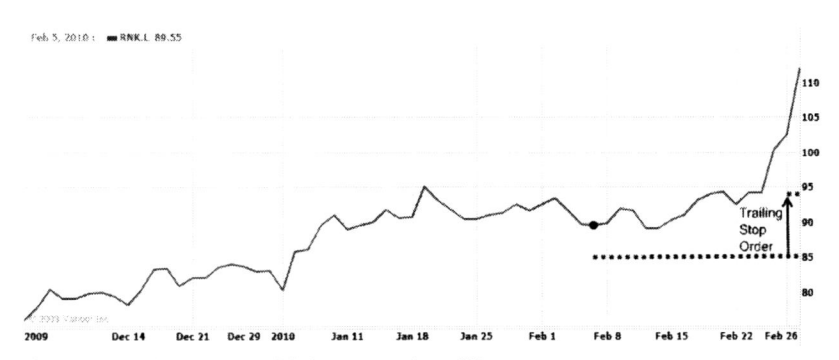

Figure 6 Rank Group Initial Stop and Trailing Stop

Automated Trailing Stops vs. Manually-Trailed Stops

In terms of trailing stops, I find one-size-fits-all automated percentage trailing stops to be somewhat problematic. I would consider a *wide* automated trailing stop in those cases where I cannot keep an eye on the market myself for an extended period of time; but otherwise I would be much more likely to trail my stop orders manually. I will aim to secure at least some profit as soon as possible, as shown above, but no sooner; ideally only when I can trail the stop to a level which is respectful of any support levels, volatility, or other stop distance criteria. Once a position is in profit, my aim is to not get stopped out at all unless absolutely necessary. Remember that as long as the price is not falling (too far), you can collect dividends while holding the position open.

A Cure for Over-Trading

My manual trailing of stop orders serves a very useful incidental purpose: it gives me 'something to do in the market'. If, like me, you have a tendency to suffer from trader's itchy fingers, you can relieve this itch by adjusting your stop orders – always up and never down on a long position – to secure more profit. It costs you nothing in trading commissions or whipsaw losses resulting from the bid-ask spread, and it really does work for me as mitigation against the risk of overtrading. Just don't go too far by ratcheting your stops orders up too tight too soon; remember that the aim should be to *not get stopped out*.

An appropriately-trailed stop order should allow you to secure some of your accrued profit without having to take the profit prematurely by selling out too soon. Some people say that you will never go broke taking a profit, but that's not necessarily true.

In a purely random system with a 50% chance of success, taking a profit of £100 on each winning trade while holding on for a loss (when you absolutely have to sell) of £1000 on each losing trade clearly *will* make you go broke. Conversely, taking a £1000 profit on each winning trade for every £100 that you lose on each losing trade would make you very rich over time – still assuming the 50/50 success rate. In position trading our aim is to maximize the gain on every winning trade (by letting profits run) and to minimize the loss on every losing trade (by cutting losses).

The Stop Order Danger Zone

I suggest not being too keen to trail an initially-tight stop order when a price begins to rise. If you want to stay in a position for a long time, like I do, then it may be better to let the stop distance widen before tailing the stop to the break-even point and beyond.

The exception to this rule is where a share price has risen a long way in a short time and is approaching a prior resistance level. The price could bounce right back down and erase the whole of the paper profit that you failed to lock-in with the stop order that you have trailed cautiously as the price rose.

The stop order danger zone begins just above the recent support price or your break-even price, and extends up to the last known resistance price. Placing your stop just inside (at the bottom of) this danger zone risks losing most or all of your potential profit and stopping out just before the prices bounces upwards again. So once you have safely moved your stop order to break-even, a big upwards price should maybe prompt you to trail your stop order more aggressively to fall not too far below the resistance level.

The price chart for Drax shown in *Figure 7 Stop Order Danger Zone* provides a good concrete example. After buying Drax at 331 on 19 May I witnessed a sharp price rise that reached about 391 on 16 June, representing a potential 60-point profit, with a pullback along the way. A stop order at 332 makes sense because this is my break-even point, the price has already tested that level, and conveniently it represents my preferred trailing stop distance of about 15%. A stop order at 369 (or higher) also makes sense because it locks-in a decent profit without crystallising the profit prematurely by simply selling. If the position stops out at this level, there is a good chance it will fall back towards support at 320 thus providing another buying opportunity. If the position doesn't stop out at this higher level, then we can shoot for the stars!

The alternative of placing your stop order within – and especially towards the bottom of – the stop order danger zone (shown grey) could result in being stopped out for *not much profit* and for *no good reason*.

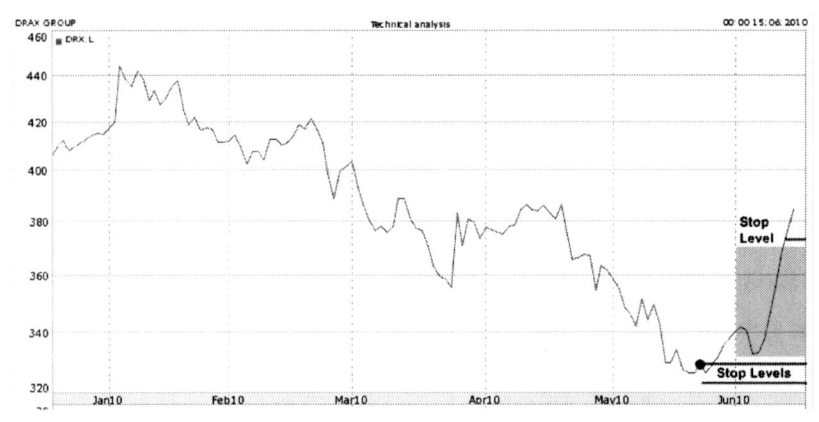

Figure 7 Stop Order Danger Zone

Guaranteed Stops and Minimum Stop Distances

Your stockbroker, CFD provider, or spread betting firm might offer you the chance to guarantee your stop orders; and you may wonder if this is a good idea.

It can be a good idea in some trading styles, and in some cases it may even work to your advantage – for example, allowing you to re-purchase a stock at a gapped-down market price that is lower than the price at which your existing position will stop out. In my 2010 Trading Trail (see *Chapter 10 – Proof of the Pudding*) the mandatory guaranteed stops did not adversely affect my results when I stuck to my *equity position trading* routine and when I avoided the temptation of wild index day-trades.

On the other hand, guaranteed stop orders usually come with a catch; either in the form of a *fee* for using them, or in the form of a *minimum stop distance* that rules out certain trading styles like rapid day-trading on stock indices or foreign exchange.

For novice traders, minimum stop distances may be beneficial in training you to trail your stop orders not too close to a rising share price.

While personally I'm fairly relaxed about whether stop orders are guaranteed or not, I would not be inclined to pay for the privilege, and the minimum stop distances can be problematic when first establishing a position with a tight stop. Minimum stop distances oblige us to accept a greater initial risk than otherwise we would like, and necessitate having to trail the stop order upwards as quickly as possible (which is labour-intensive) to the desired level.

Overcoming Minimum Stop Distances

Regardless of any minimum stop distance, you can of course close a position manually whenever you like – no matter how little the price has fallen. Thus one way to bridge the gap between your desired initial stop level and the minimum initial stop distance is to apply a mental stop; i.e. be resolved to close the position manually if you see that the price has fallen to your ideal initial stop level. This can also be very labour-intensive and mentally draining, and so should be limited to the initial period until you have trailed the minimum stop to your desired level.

Alternatively, if your trading platform allows, you could place a standalone stop order to *sell short* at your desired stop level. On most spread betting platforms, the successful execution of this order should have the effect of closing your existing long position rather than establishing a new short position.

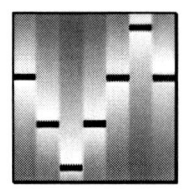

4 – On Position Sizing

The term position sizing refers to the amount of money you invest (or bet) initially, and to the size of investment (or bet stake) you maintain throughout the life of a trade while your position is open.

Good position sizing ensures that you don't bet the whole farm on one position at one time – which would be one sure way to the poor house.

Day Trader's Approach

A day trader might adopt a position sizing strategy of allocating a small percentage of his total trading budget to each discrete trade, so that he can cope with the kind of extended run of bad luck that is inevitable. By allocating say 5% (1/20th) of his trading funds to each trade, he can suffer a run of up to 19 failed trades en route to a winning trade.

In this way, a trader who trades one market (e.g. the S&P index) is using position sizing to *diversify his risk over time*.

Investor's Approach

An investor might adopt a position sizing strategy of allocating say 5% (1/20th) of her investment funds to each one of twenty separate investments. The chance of all twenty assets falling in value simultaneously is small, and the chance of all twenty investments becoming worthless – i.e. going bust – may be regarded as negligible.

In this way an investor is using position sizing to *diversify her risk across assets*.

Position Trader's Approach

As a position trader, I would take a best-of-both-worlds approach by using effective position sizing to diversify my risk *across assets* and *over time*.

Like the investor, at any one time I may have several separate stock positions in play – each one funded with a small percentage of my overall trading budget. Like a day trader, I will establish each position (place each trade) when the time is right rather than committing my entire trading budget all at once.

Although position sizing is an effective way to diversify risk across assets and over time, this chapter is not about diversification as such. That's what *Chapter 2 – On Diversification* was for.

The present chapter is primarily about not investing (or betting) too much money too soon.

Position Sizing and Stop Orders

There is an important relationship between *position sizing* and *stop orders*.

Investing with a position size of £1000 and no stop order places £1000 at risk, whereas investing with a position size of £1000 and a stop order at 20% below your purchase price places only £200 at risk. Looking at this another way: with the stop order in place you could afford to invest £5000 – a bigger position size, hence more upside potential – for no more than your original £1000 risk.

Spread betting with a position size of £10-per-point on a stock priced at 100p with no stop order places £1000 at risk, whereas spread betting with a position size of £10-per-point on a stock priced at 100p with a stop order at 80p places only £200 at risk. With the stop order in place you could afford to stake £50-per-point – a bigger position size, hence more upside potential – for no more than your original £1000 risk.

I would be less likely to increase my position size in this way, and more likely to use the notionally freed-up risk capital in order to establish additional *diversified* positions; or retain the additional risk capital as a contingency fund for *staying in the game*.

Position Sizing and "Value at Risk"

If you invest a total of £10,000 as a separate £1000 investment in each of 10 stocks, and you apply a stop-loss at minus 20% to each position, then you have placed only £2,000 of your total £10,000 tied-up capital *at risk*. Providing your stop orders execute as expected, that is. If the worst happens, the market crashes, and all your positions stop out, you will still have an £8,000 fund with which to *play again*.

With spread bets it works slightly differently in that all of the capital you tie up is *risk capital*. If you fund a spread betting account with £10,000 and establish as many positions as you can until there are no funds left for new positions, then, even with your stop orders in place, you have placed your *entire funds at risk*. If all your positions stop out, you will end up with nothing. Therefore if you wish to retain £8,000 of your £10,000 trading budget as your 'play-again' fund, you should size your positions – and place your stop orders – so that only £2,000 is at risk and your remaining £8,000 is designated as tradable funds.

This is only an example to highlight the difference between traditional investments and spread bets, so don't take it too literally. There's nothing magic about placing exactly 20% of your funds, and no more, at risk. Sometimes it will make sense to risk more; and sometimes less. But if disaster should strike, you must *live to play again*.

When not to buy

There may be times when there is no combination of share price, stop order placement, and position size that meets your money management criteria… and you will have to pass up on a candidate trade.

As a concrete example: in one of my spread betting accounts I was looking to establish a position in house-builder Bellway. With the share price at 680p, and with the spread betting platform mandating a minimum stake size of £1-per-point (no fractional bets allowed) and a mandatory minimum stop distance of 10%, the initial risk on this new position would have been £70. Since my overall total budget (i.e. the total amount I was willing to risk) was £1000, this one trade would have accounted for 7% of my total risk – which was a higher percentage than the 1%-or-so I am willing to risk on *any one position*. So I walked away.

In this scenario I could either look for a lower-priced share, or else make the trade in another account that allowed fractional position sizes or which did not mandate minimum stop distances.

Position Sizing and Options

If you're ever tempted to trade options or covered warrants – and I'm not suggesting that you do – you will most likely find that stop orders are not allowed. This means that all of the money you stake is at risk, and therefore *position sizing* (i.e. not tying up your entire trading budget) is your only defence against being taken out of the game.

Initial and Ongoing Position Size

I regard my initial positions as being somewhat exploratory, and therefore I often deploy a one-size-fits-all initial position size of always £1-per-point on a spread bet or £1000 as a traditional investment just to gain a toe-hold. It keeps things simple, and absolves me from having to make an optimal position size calculation when I need to establish a position quickly on a price gap-down.

As one of my blog followers has pointed out, this may not be the most efficient use of my capital.

A traditional investment of £1000 in a stock that rises by 20% will yield a £200 profit regardless of the original price of the stock. In contrast: a £1-per-point spread bet on a stock that rises by 20% will yield a £200 profit on a stock priced at 1000p-per-share, a £20 profit on a stock priced at 100p-per-share, and only £2 profit on a stock priced at 10p-per-share.

While personally I do not advocate performing a specific detailed calculation at the time of each investment to ensure that each spread bet is the equivalent of (for example) a £1000 investment, I do see some value in adopting the rule-of-thumb approach of betting £1-per-point on three-digit stock prices, £10-per-point on two-digit stock prices, and so on. On four-digit indices this approach would of course require the spread betting firm to accept fractional bets of £0.1-per-point. At all times this should be in the context of the overall money management criteria of risking no more than 1% (for example) of available capital on each trade.

Beware stocks priced with a multiplication factor on spread betting platforms; for example priced as 'Per Unit 0.01', which means that your £1-per-point spread bet is already the equivalent of a massive £100-per-point bet.

As you will see in the next chapter, position sizing need not be static in any case. Returns may be enhanced by increasing your position size in winning positions; in a process known as *pyramiding*. Thus my ultimate position sizes are determined by the behaviour of my stock holdings themselves. So by the time my stock position priced initially in two digits becomes a three-digit stock, I might already have increased my position size to £10-per-point through pyramiding.

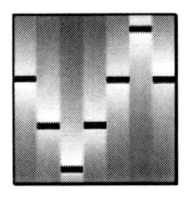

5 – On Pyramiding

I concluded the previous chapter by stating that position sizing need not be static; that returns may be enhanced by increasing your position size in winning positions using an approach known as *pyramiding*.

In this chapter I contrast the pyramiding approach with the ostensibly more logical, perhaps more widely practiced, and often more dangerous approach of 'averaging down'.

About "Averaging Down"

When you make an investment in a stock and the price subsequently falls, it can be very tempting to make an additional investment in order to *average down* your combined purchase price.

You buy £100 worth of shares of a stock priced at 100p each. When the price falls to 80p you buy an additional £100 worth of shares. Not only has your second investment bought you more shares (125 vs. 100) at the lower price of 80p, but also the share price needs to rise only to 89p rather than the original 100p in order for you to more-than *break even* at £200.25 (shown bold below) on the combined purchases.

	Share Price	Purchase Cost	Number of Shares	Value at 80p Price	Value at 89p Price	Value at 100p Price
First Purchase	100p	£100	100	£80	£89	£100
Second Purchase	80p	£100	125	£100	£111.25	£125
Total	88.9p (avg)	£200	225	£180	**£200.25**	£225

If the share price recovers its original value of 100p you make a £25 profit.

It's tempting isn't it? And for stock indices it might just work, because – to date, at least – stock indices have always recovered… eventually. But individual falling stocks do not always recover, and sometimes they go bust.

No matter how many times you average down on a single stock, and no matter how much you stand to gain if the price subsequently recovers, if the price never recovers – and instead falls to zero – then I'm afraid you've lost it all! That's what would have happened if you had averaged down on *Northern Rock* bank in the UK or *Lehman Brothers* in the USA.

On one of many positions it would be bad enough, but it gets worse because a falling stock acts like a magnet for your investment funds. Typically you close otherwise profitable positions in order to free up funds to invest in the failing stock you are averaging down.

Pyramiding and "Averaging Up"

Pyramiding is analogous to averaging up; a process in which you make additional investments as the price rises rather than as it falls, as shown in the table below.

POSITION TRADING

	Share Price	Purchase Cost	Number of Shares	Value at 100p Price	Value at 110p Price	Value at 120p Price
First Purchase	100p	£100	100	£100	£110	£120
Second Purchase	110p	£100	91		£100	£109.20
Total		£200	191	£100	£210	£229.20

A single investment at price 100p would yield £10 profit by the time the price reached 110p. With an additional investment along the way at 110p, the combined profit would be £29.20 by the time the price reached 120p.

Note that in the 'averaging down' case, the profit would be £20 on the single position (there wouldn't be a second purchase) if the price rose from 100p to 120p without falling first.

This improvement in the rise-without-a-prior-fall case comes apparently at the expense of a lower profit in the rise-after-a-fall case: £229.30 having averaged up vs. £270 (calculated as 225 shares now priced @ 120p each) having averaged down rather than up.

But think about what we are sacrificing here. In the average down case we have put £200 (and increasing) on the line with a stock that may fall all the way to zero. In the averaging up case we have put only £100 (and never any more) on the line with a stock that may fall all the way to zero.

When averaging down, the most we can lose is 'all our money'. When averaging up, the most we can lose is 'limited to our initial investment'.

Those of you who are paying attention may well have figured out that even in the averaging up scenario, we still stand to lose *all our money* if we have committed all our funds when the rising stock turns around and falls to zero. But I have an answer to this, which I'll reveal when discussing stop orders later in this chapter.

When averaging down, there would be no such answer because we would never sell out no matter how low the price went.

Real-Life Pyramiding Example

Pyramiding is best demonstrated in the context of a real-life example, such as the example of National Express Group that follows. It is also best demonstrated in the context of a spread bet, because with a £1-per-point bet any one-point upward or downward movement of the price equates to £1 of profit or loss.

Note that pyramiding is just as applicable to traditional equity investments, but the maths is a little more difficult to explain. For example, a £170 investment at a price of 170p would also give £1 of profit and loss for every one-point movement in the price. But when the price moved up to 200p we would need to make an additional £200 investment in order to maintain the same £1-per-point profit or loss.

In *Figure 8 Pyramiding into National Express* you can see how the share price increased steadily – with occasional intermittent pullbacks – between December 2009 and March 2010.

My initial £1-per-point position established at 170p in early December would have shown a profit of £15 by mid-December. By 10 January this single initial position would have shown a profit of £30, but by establishing an additional £1-per-point position at a price of 185 in mid-December I would have increased the profit on the *combined positions* to £45. By the end of February 2010 these two positions would have generated a profit of £75, but by establishing an

£1-per-point position at a price of 200 on 10 January 2010 ositions would have generated a higher profit of £90. For ie original single £1-per-point spread bet would have ofit of only £45.

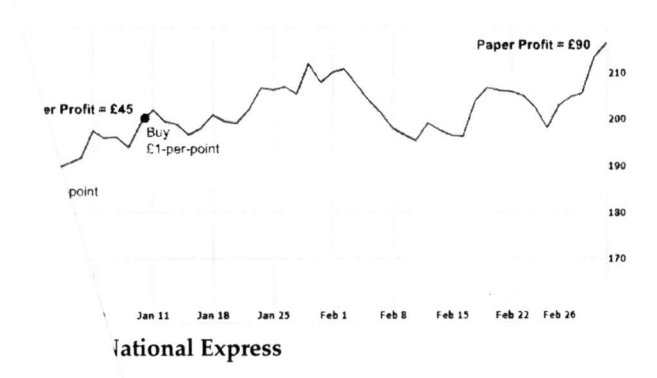

National Express

's way would have increased my overall r *profits*. As stated previously: if the share he way to zero, you lose everything! This ...in in the averaging down scenario because at least the p ɔ heading in the right direction, up, but in the markets anything can happen.

We need a way to pyramid our profits while at the same time protecting those profits (and our original capital). And this is where stop orders come in.

Pyramiding and Stop Orders

The purpose of combining *stop orders* with *pyramiding* is to ensure that every additional investment is made *with less risk*, as is demonstrated in *Figure 9 Pyramiding into National Express (with Stop Orders)*.

When placing the initial spread bet, or equivalent investment, at a price of 170p I would apply a protective stop order (in this case) at 160p thereby limiting my initial monetary risk to just £10. This is shown in the figure as *Secured Outcome* = -£10. When placing my second bet at a price of 185p I would apply a protective stop order on both positions at 175p, thereby securing a profit of £5 on the first position and accepting a risk of £10 on the second position; overall a *secured outcome* of -£5. This principle would be repeated when placing the third bet at 200p, thereby *securing* an overall profit of £15. And so on.

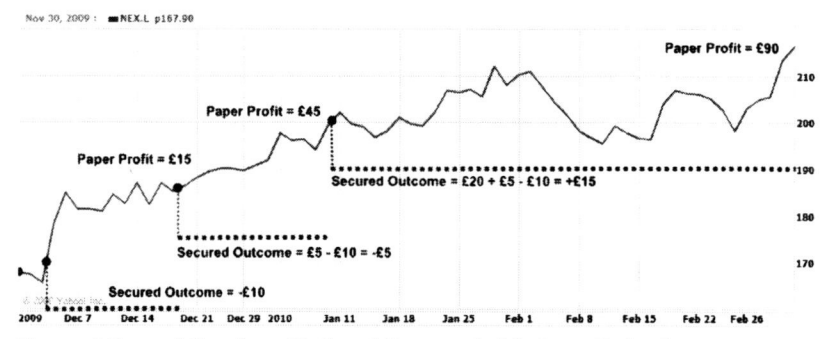

Figure 9 Pyramiding into National Express (with Stop Orders)

Think carefully about what I have achieved here. While increasing my upside potential at each stage – because I have more bets in play, or a greater investment working for me – I have at the same time *reduced my risk* or *increased my secured profit* at each stage. All thanks to the effective application of stop orders.

At any point I have the option of banking the higher *paper profit*, but I prefer not to.

Averaging Down with Stop Orders

You might wonder how you could apply stop orders to reduce risk, or secure profit, in the *averaging down* scenario. Well, you can't!

When averaging down, you purposefully hold falling positions, and in fact add to them, rather than selling them for a manageable loss. So in this case, stop orders would not help you at all.

Top-Heavy and Bottom-Heavy Pyramids

Some of you may be tempted to increase the size of your additional stakes as the pyramid grows, in order to further magnify the upside potential. But you do so at the risk of building a top-heavy pyramid that topples more easily, and in which it is more difficult to secure additional profit at the time of each investment.

It is much safer to build a bottom-heavy pyramid in which smaller additional investments are supported by a bigger base of accrued profits. One way to do this would be to invest say £5000 initially, and then £2500, and then £1250, at subsequent stages. But you might not have to.

My simple approach is to place equal £1-per-point bets at each stage so that at the second stage you are increasing your total stake by 100% (from £1-per-point to £2-per-point), at the third stage you are increasing your total stake by 50% (from £2-per-point to £3-per-point), at the fourth stage by 33.3%, and so on. So your additional investment at each stage represents a smaller proportion of your overall investment.

When making traditional investments rather than placing spread bets, I would invest an equal amount at each stage; say £1000-a-time. This is not exactly the same mathematically as placing equal-sized pounds-per-point spread bets, but it achieves a similar aim and keeps things simple.

Funding for Pyramiding

In order to pyramid into a stock position you need additional funds, and I can think of three ways of obtaining those additional funds:

- Reinvesting dividends.

- Introducing more capital, at no additional risk.

- Freeing up margin.

Reinvesting Dividends

Seasoned investors and investment web sites will tell you how beneficial it can be to reinvest your dividends. Reinvesting your dividends helps you to compound your returns, in the same way that leaving your interest payments in a savings deposit account helps to compound your gain.

At a savings rate (or dividend yield) of 5%, in Year 1 your £1000 investment becomes £1050; an increase of £50.

In Year 2 your £1050 becomes £1102.50; an increase of £52.50.

In Year 3 your £1102.50 becomes £1157.63; an increase of £55.13.

..and so on.

Over the three-year period your total return is £157.63 compared with a non-compounded rate (if you had withdrawn the interest payments) of £150. Leaving your interest receipts on deposit, or re-investing your dividends, could *double your money in ten years* at a compounded rate of 7.2% without you ever having to introduce more funds.

Beware that unlike interest receipts which only serve to *increase* your deposit balance, the capital value of a stock – as reflected by its price – is likely to fall by the dividend amount whenever a dividend becomes payable. For example: you receive a 5% dividend, but the share price falls by 5% in recognition of the fact that new investors will not be entitled to the dividend. What's the point in receiving the dividends then, you might think. And to some extent I agree with you which is why in *Chapter 8 – On Dividends* I suggest that we don't chase high-yielding stocks. But if you find yourself holding a stock that pays a dividend, it should be more profitable to re-invest it than to withdraw it.

Many schemes are available whereby your money manager will reinvest your dividends for you automatically in the same stock, same index, or same managed fund. But the same stock, index, or managed fund may not be the best place to re-invest your dividend proceeds.

My approach is to collect the dividends from several existing positions and to pyramid the combined cash into the *best prospect position*; or failing that, to open an entirely new position that represents the best prospect at the time.

Introducing More Capital, at NO Additional Risk

You might find yourself holding a portfolio of non-dividend-paying stocks, in which case you will not be able to pyramid by re-investing the dividends. You might also find that dividends accrue too slowly for you to pyramid effectively, or that those dividends appear in your account at not quite the right time.

In these cases you can pyramid into positions by introducing more new funds into your account. You need to have the spare cash, of course, but you do not necessarily have to *risk* the new cash.

Do you remember in *Figure 9 Pyramiding into National Express (with Stop Orders)* that despite putting up more cash, we actually secured more profit (and hence reduced our risk) each time we pyramided? All thanks to trailing our stop orders.

It's all well and good that we can pyramid without risking additional cash, but we still need to find the cash!

Well, one way to find the extra cash is to borrow it from a friend or family member who may be comforted by the fact that you are staking the additional money *at no additional risk*; which leads me on to…

Freeing Up Margin

You may well have an unlikely friend who will lend you additional investment funds on this no-risk basis. It's your stockbroker, your Contracts for Difference (CFD) provider, or your spread betting company.

As described in the next chapter, the provider of your trading platform might let you trade 'on margin' which basically means trading with borrowed money. In many cases the lower your assessable risk, the more money you can borrow for trading. It works something like this (refer back to *Figure 9 Pyramiding into National Express (with Stop Orders)*):

In general, spread betting platforms require you to put up an amount of money proportional to the amount you stand to lose. To keep things simple let's suppose that on your new £1-per-point position priced at 100p with a stop order at 90p, the spread betting company requires you to 'put up' or deposit £10 – calculated as (100p-90p) * £1 – in order to hold this position. If the price rises to 110p and you trail your stop order to 100p you have effectively covered your potential loss, and in most cases the spread betting company will free up your original £10 deposit so that you can risk it on another trade.

It might not work exactly like this, but I'm sure you get the idea: the more you reduce your risk by trailing your stop orders, the more your deposited funds will become *available for trading*. In these cases you should be able to pyramid *additional positions* in the same stock or different one without having to deposit *additional funds*.

Note that different trading platforms work slightly differently in this respect. On some platforms your available trading funds will increase indefinitely as you raise your stop orders on existing positions whereas on other platforms your available trading funds will increase only until your stop order has reached break-even. The latter approach is much safer since you can never risk money that you have not yet *banked* by stopping out, but it can slow down the pyramiding process.

When to Pyramid

In my earlier examples illustrated by *Figure 8 Pyramiding into National Express* and *Figure 9 Pyramiding into National Express (with Stop Orders)* I chose fairly arbitrary time to pyramid, corresponding with prices that made my calculations easier.

In reality I choose a very specific time to pyramid into an existing position: when my existing position is about to stop-out. Remember that I try to place and then trail my stops below identifiable support levels. If I establish an additional position slightly above my anticipated stop-out price, with a *tight* stop order on the new position corresponding with my original stop level, one of two things will happen:

- The market price will breech the support price, and both positions will stop-out – for a small loss on the new position, and hopefully at a profit on the existing position(s).

- Or, the price will rebound from support and I will henceforth have a bigger position working in my favour.

Aside from this specific guidance, I have a more general point to make about when to pyramid. Don't pyramid on market strength; wait for a correction. You might also know this as *buying on the dips*.

And don't forget that I will only pyramid into a position that is already in profit, and when I have sufficient unallocated risk capital.

Rebuilding a Pyramid

When a pyramid collapses (not as bad as it sounds) because all your positions have stopped out, this raises the question of whether and when to start rebuilding the pyramid. My general answer to this question would be to start rebuilding only if we can do so at lower than the last stop-out price, the lower the better, and only with the minimum position size.

Here is a concrete example:

I had established an exploratory £1-per-point position in Northgate, into which I pyramided an additional £1-per-point when the first position was showing more than enough profit to absorb the risk on the second position. To cut a long story short, both positions eventually stopped out for profits of £76.50 and £19.70 respectively.

Those positions stopped out at a price of 232 and I was able shortly afterwards to establish a new single £1-per-point position at a price of 225.6. So, I had banked a total £96.20 profit on my original pyramided positions and I had notionally saved an additional £6.40 by re-establishing my single new position at a lower price than the price at which I stopped out. My initial risk on the new position was rather high at £17 (with a new stop order at 209) but within a day I had trailed this to better than break-even at 226.

This demonstrates how the pyramiding cycle is meant to play out.

Beware Overweight Pyramids

Just as I try to diversify my risk across many positions, I also try to diversify my risk ultimately across many pyramids. In its simplest form I would seek to pyramid equally across the board such that I would have moved all of my £1-per-point positions up to £2-per-point before moving any of them up to £3-per-point. In its more complex form I would seek to pyramid my low-price stocks quicker than my high-priced stocks.

This approach to equalising my pyramids will *not maximise the profit potential* which may well be better maximised by piling aggressively into the higher priced stocks, but it will help to *minimise risk.*

At one point in the Trading Trail blog I had pyramided a stock priced at 230 up to £3-per-point. Although there was no risk in the sense that my combined positions would exit at a net profit, imagine what would have happened if the price had gapped down massively or the stock had gone bust overnight. It does happen, and if it did I would have lost some £600-£700 which would have been a big deal – possibly fatal – in my puny £1000 demonstration account. In traditional stock market lingo, I was very overweight in this position as a proportion of my total portfolio risk.

However low the *probability* of a bad outcome is, if the *impact* is high then the *risk* is high. Note that the true definition of speculative risk is:

```
risk = probability x impact
```

While I'm not a nervous flyer, this is why air travel doesn't feel quite right to me. The chance of being involved in a plane crash may be low, but if it happens... I'm dead!

Non-Specific Pyramiding

As described here: pyramiding means using accrued profits to increase our stakes specifically in existing positions. But there is another more general way to think about pyramiding; which is using accrued profits to increase the size of our stakes in new positions as well as existing ones.

If our trading account grows in size by 100%, from a £1000 initial trading budget to a £2000 portfolio value, we might consider ourselves justified in opening all new positions at £2-per-point (or with a £2000 initial investment) rather than the original £1-per-point (or £1000 investment).

I call this non-specific pyramiding.

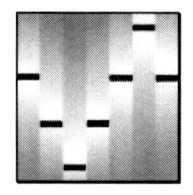

6 – On Leverage

Leverage is the means by which you can amplify the gains you make on a rising price. It is also the means by which you can amplify the losses you make on a falling price – so be careful. The two chapters, *Chapter 3 – On Stop Orders* and *Chapter 4 – On Position Sizing*, presented two mechanisms for 'being careful' by utilising stop orders and prudent position sizing. These safety mechanisms become even more important, even vitally so, when you employ leverage.

What is leverage?

You may be familiar with the idea of a physical *lever*, which magnifies the effect of you muscle power. A correctly positioned lever will help you to lift an item twice as heavy, maybe even ten times as heavy, as you could normally lift.

Financial leverage works the same way. A leveraged product such as the ProShares Ultra DOW 30 ETF aims to generate 2x the return of the Dow Jones index. So if the index rises by 10% you would expect your investment to increase by 20%. In a sense, your investment would be lifting twice its own weight.

Note that *covered warrants* and other *options* also provide leverage such that your gains – and potential losses, don't forget – are amplified. However, I generally (but not always) steer clear of options in my position-trading strategy for two very good reasons:

- My stockbroker does not allow me to place stop orders on options.

- These financial instruments have an expiry date; which means that they cannot be held for the ideal holding period of 'forever'.

Leverage and Margin

In many cases leverage is achieved through the use of margin, by which you put down a sum of money in order to control a larger notional investment. The easiest way to think about this is in terms of your home loan.

When purchasing a house for £100,000, you might typically contribute £20,000 (i.e. 20%) as a deposit and borrow the remaining £80,000 (i.e. 80%) from a bank in the form of a mortgage. Thus your £20,000 contribution allows you effectively to gain control of a £100,000 asset. If house prices increased by 10% in one year, the value of your asset would have increased by £10,000; or, to put it another way, you would have achieved a massive 50% return on your original £20,000 investment in one year.

Of course, this is all thanks to the bank lending you four times the amount of money you actually put down, thus giving you 5-times leverage. But banks are not charities, so you will be charged a fee in the form of mortgage interest. As long as your cost of financing (paying the interest, at maybe 5%) is lower than the price appreciation of the asset (10% in this example, remember) you will make money.

But there's more.

In the 1990s and early 2000s in the UK and many other countries, *buy-to-let* property speculation was very popular. A property speculator would finance a house purchase in exactly the way just described, but crucially they would not live in the house. They would rent the house to someone else, and would use the rental income to pay the cost of financing – i.e. to pay the mortgage interest. By doing so, they would pocket the full 50% return on their £20,000 investment; on paper, at least.

So now you're thinking: what does this have to do with stocks?

Well, imagine if your stockbroker would allow you to purchase £10,000 worth of stock using a £2,000 deposit; effectively loaning you £8,000 in the process. If the broker charged you 5% annually on this loan, and the stock in question generated 5% in dividends then you would effectively achieve a 5-times gain on any stock price appreciation at no additional cost. If the stock price increased by 10%, your investment would increase by 50%. Some stockbrokers and most if not all spread betting and CFD firms will allow you to do exactly this.

Warning: *This amplifying effect also works in reverse. It would take a price fall of only 20% to wipe out your £2,000 deposit and cause the broker to ask you for more money by making a* **margin call***. Upon receiving a margin call, you would need to put up (extra cash) or shut up (close the position for the £2,000 loss). Most successful traders recommend closing your positions rather than throwing good money after bad by meeting a margin call.*

Spread Betting

In the UK and some other jurisdictions (notably not the USA) it is possible to place leveraged trades as *spread bets* with a spread betting provider.

For example, my spread betting provider allows me to place a £1-per-point spread bet on the Germany 30 (DAX) index, which as I write stands at a price of 5795. It means that I will *win* (or profit by) £1 for every one point that the index rises. In order to achieve this same return with a traditional investment, I would need to have £5795 available for investment, yet the spread betting provider does not oblige me to deposit anything like that amount.

Note that if the entire German economy goes down the pan and its stock index falls to zero, the spread betting provider will ask you for the full £5795, which is why it is so important to apply a stop order (*Chapter 3 – On Stop Orders*) to limit your downside risk on leveraged spread bets. But the point is that if the index only ever rises after you place the bet, then you need never have had the full £5795 available at all; only enough to cover the *margin*, the partial investment down-payment demanded by the spread betting company.

There may be another way in which the gains and losses on spread bets are magnified, which is when the spread bet is not on a per-point (or per-pence) basis. For example, one of my spread betting providers currently specifies bets in Swedbank (a Swedish bank) as *Per Unit 0.01*, which means that a one-point (or one pence) rise or fall in the share price will generate a £100 profit or loss on my £1-per-point spread bet rather than the £1 profit or loss that you might expect. Look out for that situation, as it's tripped me up a few times by forcing me to take on much more risk than I intended.

Leveraged Options

One of the problems when running the position trading strategy in a regular brokerage account is the dealing charges relative to the size of your investment and anticipated return.

For example: when purchasing £1000 worth of equity in the UK you might pay a £12 transaction fee plus 0.5% stamp duty, which means your holding will be down by 1.7% before it goes anywhere. By trading *options* – for example in the form of *covered warrants* – rather than stocks in your regular brokerage account you should escape the stamp duty charge.

There is another advantage. Whereas the spread on a spread bet might also be in the order of 1.7% (or more), you have the benefit of *leverage* on any gain that you make, and the same is true of options. The initial built-in loss of a few percentage points will be more bearable if you make back 10-times your initial stake rather than 1.5-times your initial stake.

Although leveraged options may more attractive than straight equity holdings as positions in a regular brokerage account, there are some problems:

- You might not find a suitable option on the particular equity you wish to hold, particularly for smaller capitalisation stocks.

- Your regular brokerage account may well not allow stop orders on options, which means that you need to be ever vigilant and ever more cautious about position sizing.

- Options can expire worthless before your position has had chance to realise its potential, thus making long-dated options more appealing in this approach.

With those caveats in mind, it may be possible to take advantage of leverage in a regular brokerage accounts by holding positions in *options*. And I should also mention that options allow you to hold a *short position* in a regular brokerage account, which you might not be able to do otherwise.

What leverage is not

Let me set the record straight by clarifying what leverage *is not*. It is not the same as achieving double the return (in absolute terms) by investing twice as much cash in the first place, any more than a physical lever helps you to lift twice as much weight because you got twice as strong yourself by eating protein powder. It is about gaining twice as much profit (or more) *in percentage terms* from *the same amount of investment power*. Or, we must not forget, *twice as much loss* (or more).

Making a Little go a Long Way

Leveraging to the hilt is greedy and in many cases doomed to failure. Prudent leveraging is a way of "making a little go a long way" rather like adding milk to your mashed potatoes. With £1,000 leveraged up to £10,000 – for example in a spread betting account – I can achieve the same degree of diversification (establish as many separate positions) as I could with the flat £10,000. So with £10,000 to invest I would be less inclined to leverage it up to the investment power of £100,000; and more inclined to leverage £1,000 of it up to £10,000 while depositing the balance of £9,000 in the highest interest bank account I could find.

Is Leverage Dangerous?

Leverage can be risky in the sense that it amplifies your potential losses as well as gains; and for this reason some investment 'experts' advise against it.

In concrete terms: when leveraged at 20:1 a 5% move in your favour will generate a 100% profit, but a 5% move against you will *wipe you out*!

However; just as there are no dangerous cars or dogs, only dangerous drivers or owners, leverage need not be dangerous in responsible hands. The responsible user of leverage would always apply stop orders in conjunction with prudent position sizing as described in the previous chapters.

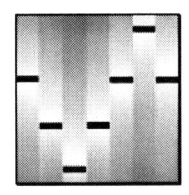

7 – On Stock Picking

Early in this book I suggested that clever stock picking is perhaps the least important aspect of the position trading approach. What I meant was that however good your stock picks are – and whether those stock picks come from hot tips, careful fundamental analysis, or from any other source – these stock picks will count for nothing if you do not practice sound *money management* through effective *position sizing* and *stop order placement.*

How many times have you invested in a sure-fire prospect stock only to be disheartened when its share price falls soon after purchase? How many times have you sold out in panic only to see the price recover, or even worse, held on for the recovery that never comes. How many times have you seen the price of your hot stock rocket as expected, and then watched passively as the price falls back... and eventually goes into loss?

Not to be too pessimistic here, once your money management regime has become second nature then it will obviously be beneficial to pick the right stocks at the right time. The true power of leverage and pyramiding will be realized by investing in those stocks that have the highest reward / risk ratio.

On Position Entry

This chapter might just as well have been titled *On Position Entry,* because the techniques described here – on when and how to establish new positions based on price action – need not be limited to stocks. The techniques might be adapted for market indices, commodities, and other financial instruments that have constantly fluctuating prices.

But I promised you a chapter on *Stock Picking*, so here we go.

The What and When of Stock Picking

Many trading authors distinguish between *what* you should buy, and *when* you should buy it. There may be some merit in screening for stocks on some *fundamental* criteria, and then watching them for the optimal time to dive in based on *technical* price action.

In my approach, I tend to distil the 'what' and 'when' of stock picking into simply *when*. If the short-term price action tells me that it may be a good time to purchase a stock in anticipation of an immediate upturn (however small), and if the longer-term price chart implies a potentially large upside potential, then I will establish an exploratory position on the basis that the price alone tells me everything I need to know.

For me, the 'what' and 'when' of stock picking is something of an artificial distinction. A particular stock (the 'what') is the right one to buy if *now* (the 'when') is the right time to buy it.

The Living Watch List and the Stop-Out List

I do retain the notion of a *watch list*, but not in the sense of a list of pre-selected stocks I am watching with a view to purchasing them in future. I put a stock onto my watch list by establishing an exploratory position in that stock with a small *position size*. Thus my portfolio is itself my watch list – which also explains why I hold so many positions simultaneously. The subsequent price behaviour of the stocks on this *living watch list* determines which positions attract more of my capital ultimately through the process of *pyramiding*.

As will be described later, I also hold the notion of a *Stop-Out List*: a list of stocks that I have sold previously (by stopping out) and which I hope to purchase at a later date at a lower price.

> 2nd Edition Note: In the 1st edition of this book, I called it my "Sold List". The new term "Stop-Out List" makes it direction-agnostic and therefore potentially of use to 'short' position traders who might look to SELL at a higher price than the last stop-out price.

This *Stop-Out List* is more analogous to the traditional *watch list* (of pre-selected stocks I am not currently holding, but hope to in the future) with one important distinction: these stocks *were* previously held in my portfolio and hence could previously be found on my *living watch list*. I did not screen for them according to fundamental ratios or any other non-price-action criteria.

If you have a watch list of stocks that you pre-select based on company fundamentals or other criteria, you don't need to throw the list away. It simply means that you will have a smaller pool of candidate stocks than I do – but, you will hope, of better quality.

In some ways my *Sold List* (let's assume I'm a long trader) represents the 'ones that got away', the stocks in which I wish I still had a position because the price has not yet fallen below – and may even have risen significantly above – my last stop-out price. But I've learnt not to feel bad about this. You'd be surprised at how often a stock rises up from your last stop-out price, sometimes significantly, and yet still ultimately falls back through it. If some do 'get away', so what? There are plenty more fish in the sea and (to mix my metaphors) another one will be along in a minute.

Buying on Short-Term Price Action

In this approach, the aim is to establish an initial position in a stock by buying when the price falls – suddenly, and far. The ideal time to buy is when the price has gapped or spiked down on a possible over-reaction; therefore the price may well enjoy a subsequent and immediate bounce back up. Although I'm in a position hopefully for the long term, I'd prefer to move into profit rather than loss soon after purchase.

Beware prices that have gapped up or down for purely technical reasons, such as a share-split or consolidation, in which case the stock's value is totally unaffected. Beware also that a stock price will likely gap-down for purely technical reasons on its ex-dividend date, by the amount of the dividend, merely to reflect the fact that future investors will not receive the dividend payment that existing investors will enjoy.

Figure 10 Shanks Group 5 Day Chart shows that by catching the bottom of the Shanks Group price gap-down of about 20% on Tuesday 9 March (at about 95p) we could have banked an immediate rebound profit of between 10% (price peak 105p the same day) and 15% (price peak 110p the following day).

This is not the profit I am looking for as a position trader, unless I establish a double-size initial position – e.g. a £2,000 initial investment or a £2-per-point spread bet – and choose to close out half of the position for an immediate profit while leaving the other half of the position to run potentially forever.

POSITION TRADING

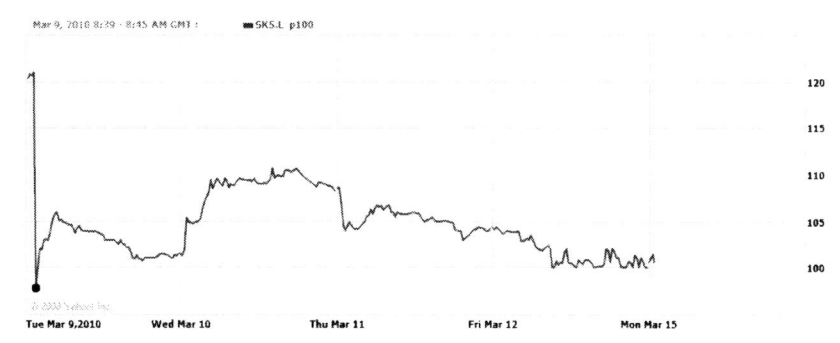

Figure 10 Shanks Group 5 Day Chart

I find these gapped-down stocks by referring to one of the *Biggest Fallers* lists provided on my stockbroker's web site or by *Yahoo! Finance*. You can find the biggest fallers in the UK, USA, and European markets at these web addresses:

FTSE All Share Price % Losers at http://uk.finance.yahoo.com/losers?e=ftas

NYSE Price % Losers at http://uk.finance.yahoo.com/losers?e=nq

NASDAQ Price % Losers at http://uk.finance.yahoo.com/losers?e=o

EuroStoxx 50 Price % Losers at http://uk.finance.yahoo.com/losers?e=stoxx50e

Anticipating the Gap

The tactic just outlined is to establish an exploratory long position after a stock's price has 'gapped-down'. In some cases we may be able to anticipate an out-of-hours price gap by analysing the pre-close price behaviour.

I can't prove this statistically, but anecdotally I can tell you that when a share price ramps up just before the close-of-play on a day that results are to be announced, it could be a portent of an overnight gap-down ahead. On 18 October 2010, after falling back throughout the day, Apple shares staged a half-day recovery to more-or-less retake the day's opening high price as shown in *Figure 11 Apple 5 Day Price Chart to 18 October 2010.*

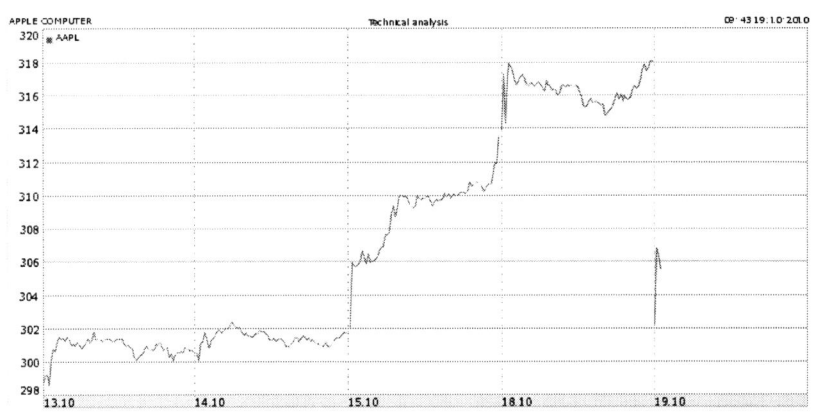

Figure 11 Apple 5 Day Price Chart to 18 October 2010

This might, just might, be the insiders' way of leaving the amateurs out-of-position by encouraging them to go long or by stopping out their short positions shortly before causing – or at least allowing – the price to gap down after the closing bell. In this specific example, the shares promptly fell by 7% during out-of-hours trading in response to a news announcement.

You may think that in the Position Trading strategy we don't need to anticipate price gaps because we always react to them. But imagine this scenario in reverse: a share price drifting down in the few hours before an overnight announcement. It might be a good time to go long so as to benefit from the initial boost of a potential overnight price gap 'up'. And in the case of Apple, it may have been a good time to establish an exploratory *short* position trade especially when you consider also the bubble-like longer term price chart (and short profit potential) shown in *Figure 12 Apple 10 Year Price Chart to 18 October 2010*.

POSITION TRADING

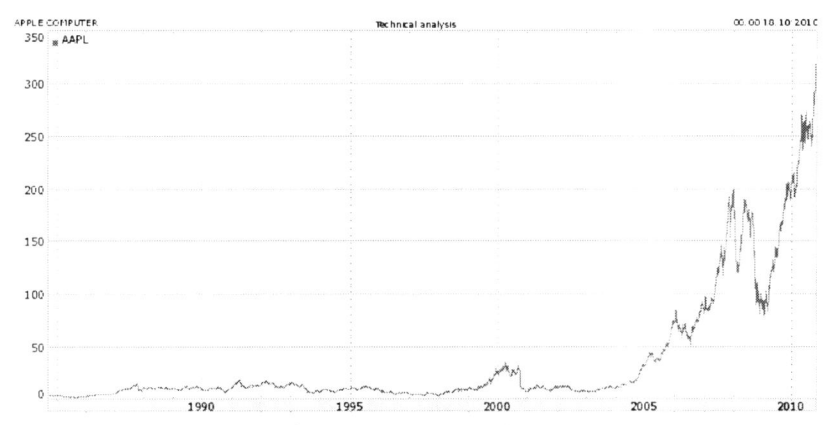

Figure 12 Apple 10 Year Price Chart to 18 October 2010

Thinking about the prospect of selling Apple short prompts me to say a little more about...

Shorting and Hedging

A position that I held in Qinetiq stopped out as a result of the 20% price gap-down shown in *Figure 13 Qinetiq 5 Year Price Chart to 2010-10-19*. You can see that price recovered almost immediately so I need not have stopped out at all.

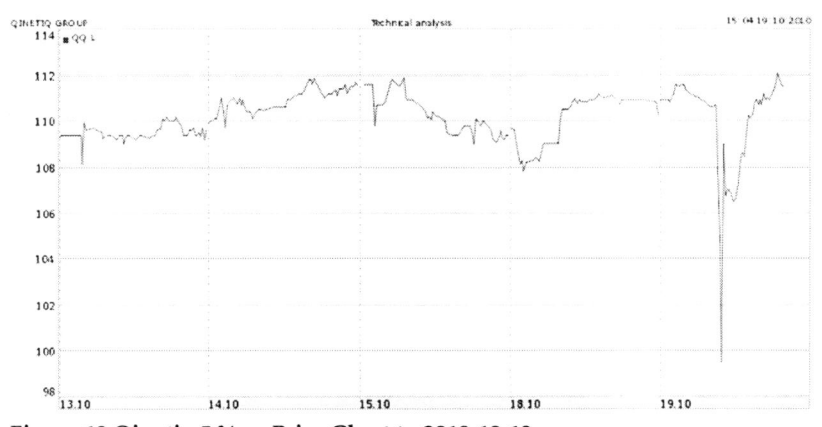

Figure 13 Qinetiq 5 Year Price Chart to 2010-10-19

In this case I was in no rush to re-establish a long position and therefore take a *whipsaw loss*. On the basis that there may be no 20%

price-drop 'smoke' without a significant 'fire', and with some apparent resistance at the pre- and post-drop price, I concluded that a short trade would be more likely to pay off. So I established a new £1-per-point *short* position at a price of 111 with a stop order at 119 for an £8 risk.

If the price of this stock fell I would trail the stop order down, and maybe even pyramid my short position, in a complete reversal of the position trading strategy.

These situations raise the possibility of holding a mixture of long and short position trades in the same account, although I'll suggest later why I think it might be advisable to hold long and short positions in separate accounts – to avoid confusion.

In the case of my Qinetiq trade, the plot thickens because in one of my spread betting accounts the original long trade had – against all the odds – not stopped out at all. Yet I fancied the short trade.

Unlike some trading platforms, the platform in question allowed me to hold a long and a (new) short position simultaneously in the same stock without one position cancelling out the other. So I hedged my long position in Qinetiq with a short position in... Qinetiq.

After this minor detour down the road of short trading and hedging, let's return to the main topic of long trading.

Buying on Market Weakness

Although the aim is to buy an individual stock based on its own individual (downwards) price action, it does no harm at all to do so at a time of overall market weakness thus giving you two opportunities for the price to go up:

- Because the price of the stock itself has over-reacted downwards, and rebounds.

- Because the market as a whole rises; and we all know that a rising tide (usually) lifts all boats.

Thus I tend to go looking for buying opportunities during periods of market weakness, and I exercise more caution during period of market strength.

Buying for Long Term Potential

While looking for stocks that have suffered a short-term price correction, it is also beneficial to zoom out to a longer term price chart. This tells you not only how the present price correction fits into the overall scheme of things, but also tells you how much upside potential there may be.

A look at the longer-term chart shown in *Figure 14 Shanks Group 5 Year Chart* tells us that this stock, now priced at less than 100p, was priced at more than 250p two years earlier in 2007. It may not be *probable* that this stock will recover to realize the apparent 150% upside, but the chart proves that it is at least *possible* because investors did once believe this stock to be worth the higher price.

Figure 14 Shanks Group 5 Year Chart

It's a more minor point (for me) but you will notice that the price has been in an uptrend – higher highs and higher lows – during the year leading up to 9 March 2010.

Risk and Reward

One of the keys to successful trading is to assess the risk you are taking (in terms of the money you could lose if your judgment is wrong) against the reward you hope to receive if you are right.

As you can see in *Figure 15 Bloomsbury 5 Year Chart*, on 22 March Bloomsbury was priced at about 115p – just above its support level of 110p that stretches back to 2007. With a stop order at 105p, the risk on this trade would be 10 points – or just £10 on a £1-per-point spread bet. There are several potential profit targets corresponding with previous high prices: one at 140p (profit potential £25), one at 175p (profit potential £60), and the long-term target of more than 350p (profit potential £235).

Target 1 Reward / Risk is 25:10, or 2.5:1

Target 2 Reward / Risk is 60:10, or 6:1

Target 3 Reward / Risk is 235:10, or 23.5:1

Even on the lowest reward / risk assumption, we can suffer 2.5 failed trades like this one for every such winning trade and still break even; in which case we need a minimum success rate of only 30% winning trades.

By letting our profits run to their full potential we may be able to suffer 23.5 failed trades like this for every one such winning trade; in which case we need a success rate of only 4% winning trades.

The more money we can make on each winning trade (by running our profit), and the less we can lose on each losing trade (by cutting our loss), the lower our *success rate* needs to be.

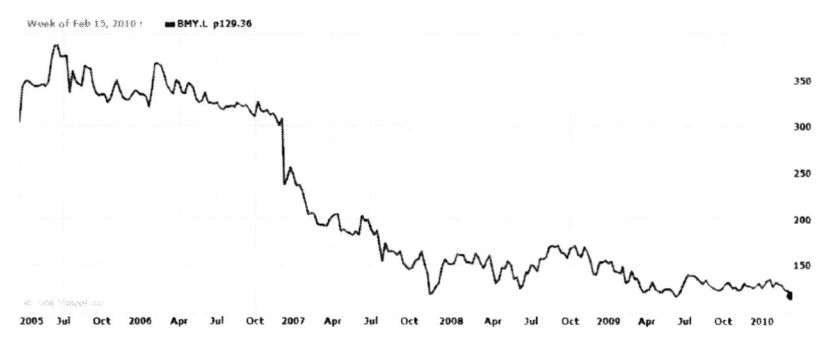

Figure 15 Bloomsbury 5 Year Chart

The important point to make here is that any trade we place must have a good reward / risk ratio. Risking £1 to make between £2.50 and £23.50 (or even more) – as indicated here – would be good. But on another hypothetical trade, risking £23.50 (if we employed a very wide initial stop order) to make only £1 (if the price was only one point away from an all-time high) would be bad.

Multiple Profit Targets and Partial Close-Outs

So which of the three profit targets should we be aiming for? The obvious answer is to aim for the highest profit target by running our profit for as long as possible, thus reducing the proportion of successful trades we must make.

This is the ideal position trading strategy, which requires a great deal of discipline and very careful trailing of stop orders. But here's another idea: the *partial close-out*, which would play out as follows:

- Imagine that we place a £4-per-point spread bet initially at 115p with a 10-point stop, thus making our initial risk £40.

- When the price hits our first target price of 140p, we sell £1-per-point in order to bank a profit of £25; thereby reducing our risk to just £15 (£40 minus £25) without having to trail our stop order. *We might also trail the stop order so as to reduce our risk even more, but let's ignore that for now.*

- When the price hits our second target price of 175p, we sell another £1-per-point in order to bank an additional profit of £60; thereby reducing our risk still further to *minus £45* (i.e. a minimum profit of £45). *Again without having to trail our stop order, but we might do so.*

- When the price hits our third target price of 350p we sell a further £1-per-point, banking yet more profit and leaving £1-per-point to run potentially indefinitely.

Note that in a regular brokerage account we might execute this strategy by making a £4000 investment initially and then closing out one-quarter of our share-holding at each price target.

As I have stressed throughout, we might also trail our stop order(s) as we go thereby reducing risk and securing profits even quicker.

Partial Close Out, or Pyramid?

The partial close-out technique just described represents an alternative to pyramiding: in the pyramiding case you add to a position as the price rises, in the partial close-out case you remove from a position as the price rises, and in both cases you are managing risk and securing profits.

I should say at this point that partial close-out is <u>not</u> the true opposite of pyramiding. Although we may reduce our position size as the price rises, we will under no circumstances 'average down' by increasing our position size as the price falls. If the price falls, we stop out. Full Stop!

When deciding whether to use the partial close-out approach or the pyramiding approach you will need to consider your *initial risk*, the potential for *freeing up trading funds*, the *visibility of profit targets*, and whether the two techniques are actually *mutually exclusive* at all.

Initial Risk

Your *initial risk* in the above example would be four times higher when using the partial close-out technique; e.g. £40 initial risk (position size £4-per-point) vs. £10 initial risk (position size £1-per-point). With a small account size it may be better to have four positions each with an initial risk of £10 (the pyramiding approach) than to have only one position with an initial risk of £40 (the partial close-out approach). In a sufficiently well-funded account, you could of course have four positions each having an initial risk of £40.

Freeing Up Trading Funds

You might also consider whether the account you are trading rewards you for locking-in profits using stop orders. In a spread betting account you should be able to free up trading funds by raising your stop order(s) to reduce your risk, but in a regular brokerage you probably can't; although your capital-at-risk is lower, you can't actually get at the cash. By locking-in profits using the partial close-out technique in your regular brokerage account, you free up real cash sooner for investment in other positions.

Visibility of Profit Targets

It is really only beneficial to implement the partial close-out approach if the chart shows clear points – i.e. resistance levels – where it may be beneficial to take some of your money off the table in anticipation of the price falling back.

Tony Loton

If you don't know what a 'resistance level' is, take a look at Appendix A – Support and Resistance... and then come back here.

Where you see both a swing-trade and a position-trade opportunity in a stock chart, it may be appropriate to invest or bet twice your usual initial stake. You close out half the position at the top of the swing and leave half your position to run.

This may be applicable over any trading timescale, even down to that of a day trader. As shown in *Figure 16 FTSE 100, 2x Day Trade*: a day trader might establish a £2-per-point long position at 11.15am after the double-bottom formation, close out half the position at or around the first profit target of 5145 (for the ultra-short-term swing), and leave the remaining £1-per-point long position to run for as long as possible until either a) the second profit target is reached at 5200, or b) the trading day ends.

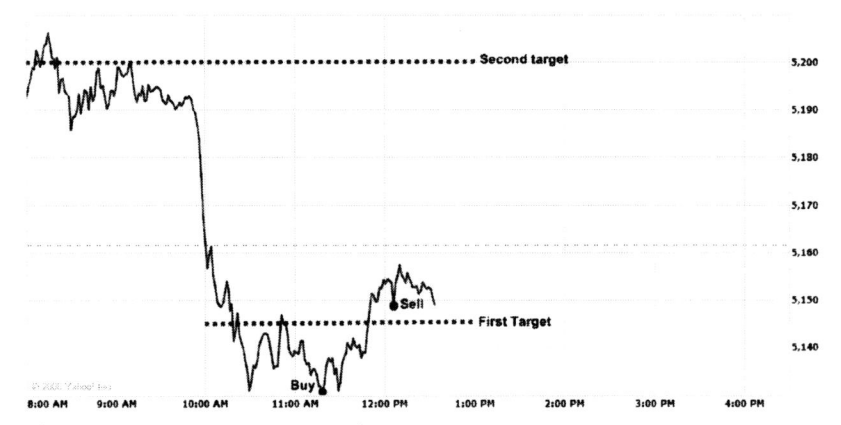

Figure 16 FTSE 100, 2x Day Trade

Whereas an orthodox day trader would close out the residual position at the second profit target, or at the end of the trading day (whichever came first), as a position trader I would be inclined do something different. After reducing my initial risk by closing out half of my position at the first profit target, I would use a manually-trailed stop order to lock-in an increasing amount of profit up to – and beyond – the second profit target.

Unlike the day trader who places big bets on small moves, I would not feel compelled to close my small residual position at the end of the day out of fear of an overnight price gap. I aim to leave something in play indefinitely because...

"A long-term investment is a short-term trade gone well!"

In this way I bridge the apparently unbridgeable gap between *buying like a trader* and *holding like an investor*.

Mutually Exclusive?
In some sense you don't have to choose between partial close-out and pyramiding. You can use both; each at the right time.

Once you have closed-out enough of a position to leave only your minimum stake in play (e.g. a £1-per-point spread bet or a £1000 investment), for example in the 'swing trade plus position trade' scenario just described, then if the price goes even higher into uncharted territory there is really only one thing you can do: *pyramid*.

If your account is of insufficient size to risk more than your minimum stake size on any one position, for fear of being under-diversified, then you must pyramid initially until you have positions at multiples of your minimum stake size. Only then will you have the option to partially close-out.

Low Price Means Low Risk

From a reward-risk perspective it should be obvious that the lower the price compared with the historic high price, the more upside potential for the position. But now I'd like to focus not on relative low prices but on absolute low prices.

When placing a pounds-per-point spread bet or CFD trade, a low absolute share price means a low risk even in the absence of a stop order. Betting £1-per-point on Yell Group at a price of 33p is less risky in terms of the total amount you could lose than a £1-per-point bet on the FTSE 100 index at a price of 5000. In the first case you would risk only £33, and in the second case you would risk £5000.

With a trading budget of £5000 you could establish only one FTSE 100 position without a stop order, but you could establish 150 Yell-Group-like positions.

In reality (if you've been paying attention) you will apply stop orders to all your positions; thus increasing the number of positions your portfolio can hold but in the same proportions as just mentioned: e.g. 2 x FTSE 100 positions vs. 300 Yell-like positions.

The bottom line here is that in a small spread betting account that does not accept fractional positions I would favour low-priced shares in order to allow for greater diversification.

Note that when making a traditional investment, of say £500, in a position in a regular brokerage account, rather than betting on a pounds-per-point basis, finding low-absolute-price shares does not matter because your risk is determined by the size of your investment rather than the share price. It may even be beneficial to focus on higher priced shares in a regular brokerage account so as to avoid this sorry scenario:

In a spread betting account I established a £1-per-point position in Real Estate Opportunities at a price of 13 with a token stop order at 3. The price dropped like a stone, and I lost £10. No big deal.

Now imagine that I had established the same position in a regular brokerage account, and lost a massive 77% when the position stopped out!

Catching a Falling Knife with the Sold List

Question: What do I do when an existing position stops out?

Answer: I add it to my *Sold List* as a potential repurchase at a lower price.

> 2nd Edition Note: I now prefer the term 'Stop-Out List' that is direction-agnostic and therefore potentially useful to 'short' position traders, but the original term 'Sold List' is more intuitive in the context of the paragraphs that follow.

Not all closed stock positions go onto my Sold List as potential buy-backs, if – for example – I think the shares have run their course and are now over-valued. But if a position stops out soon after my initial purchase and still looks like good value in the long run, I will add it to the list with a view to re-establishing my position if the price falls even further.

On my Sold List I need only two pieces of information as a minimum: the name of the stock, and the price at which I last sold it by being stopped out. The list is therefore as simple as this:

```
Begbies @ 78

Mouchel @ 189

AGA @ 118

Home Retail @ 253.55
```

> 2nd Edition Note: I now use the Stop-Out List tab of my Position Trading Cockpit spreadsheet discussed in *Chapter 11 – Automating the Strategy* instead.

Some people have compared my strategy of re-establishing my positions at lower and lower prices with *trying to catch a falling knife*, which you might have heard is one of the cardinal sins of stock speculation. But here's the difference: I only do this with my small initial position size, which is a mere fraction of the ultimate position size I hope to achieve through pyramiding.

A reader of my *Trading Trail* blog also pointed out that continually buying back at a not-much-better price would be analogous to holding the original position and simply lowering my stop order – which is also a trading no-no. Technically this may be true, but no-one forces me to re-establish my position, and I only do so having had the opportunity to reassess the merits of the trade. Stopping-out forces me to make this reassessment.

Note that in the absence of any other compelling reason to re-purchase a specific stock; I will pick a stock from my Sold List only if I can re-establish my position at a significantly lower price: the lower, the better.

So if my stock purchase at 100p stops out at 90p for a loss of £10 on a £1-per-point spread bet, and I see an opportunity later to re-purchase at 50p, I have notionally gained £40 of potential profit – calculated as (90-50)*£1 – by not holding the stock from 90p all the way down to 50p. And I can always 'average up' as the price rises from 50p back up to 100p, which leaves me not much worse off than if I had dangerously 'averaged down' to 50p.

Where *guaranteed stops* are employed there may be some rare times at which it is beneficial to stop-out and then re-establish a position immediately so as to realise a *whipsaw profit*.

Whipsaw Profits

You may have heard of *whipsaw* losses: those losses that you notch up by being stopped out at the lower *bid* price, repurchasing at the higher *ask* price, and possibly suffering an additional transaction charge to boot – and that's without even considering the additional loss you suffer if the price has rebounded upwards after you have been stopped out and before you repurchase.

POSITION TRADING

One of the benefits of *guaranteed stops* is that these can in some cases lead to the opposite of whipsaw losses; i.e. *whipsaw profits*. If a price gaps down such that the broker must stop you out at your guaranteed level, but you can repurchase immediately in the market at a lower price, then you stand to make a whipsaw profit. In this scenario, the broker who guaranteed your stop order takes the corresponding whipsaw loss.

This is not theoretical, but actual. In the course of my Trading Trail public trading experiment I made such whipsaw profits on Prudential (2 March 2010) and Shanks Group (9 March 2010) on the price gap-downs shown in *Figure 17 Prudential 2 March Price Gap Down* and *Figure 18 Shanks Group 9 March Price Gap Down*.

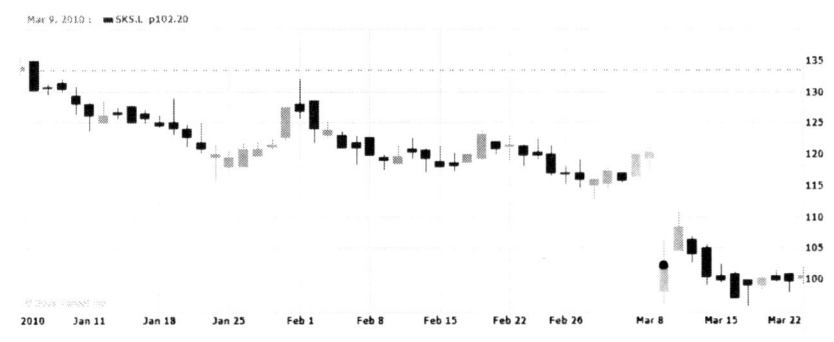

Figure 17 Prudential 2 March Price Gap Down

Figure 18 Shanks Group 9 March Price Gap Down

I really only enjoyed a whipsaw profit in these cases because:

- the price rose (so as to begin closing the gap) immediately after my re-purchase

- my spread betting provider offered free guaranteed stops

- spread betting attracts no transaction fees other than the bid-ask spread

- the spread on these particular stocks was so tight

It's a tall order for all of these things to be true, but as I have demonstrated, it's not impossible.

When to Buy Higher, and When Not to Buy Lower

Taken in its purest form, my approach suggests that we should <u>never</u> re-establish a long position at higher price than our last stop-out price. I do break this rule sometimes, ever so slightly, and when I think it is prudent to do so. A good example of this was the Micro Focus trade that I blogged about on 18 August 2010:

I decided to re-purchase Micro Focus at a price of 277.3, which was actually slightly higher than my last stop-out price of 275. My justification was that the price has gone horizontal for the last three days so there was a good case for a new initial stop order at 269p. I felt comfortable *buying higher* because the numbers were so small: it was only 2 points (<1%) more expensive than at my stop-out price and I was taking on only £8 new risk which was less than 1% of my trading capital.

In this case I considered that getting back in position on a stock with significant upside potential was worth the minimal risk of *buying higher*.

When a stock's price does fall below the last stop-out price, some people have asked how long we should wait before re-purchasing. Is

1% a sufficient discount? What about 5%, 10%, or even 30%? The previous example illustrates that there is no one-size-fits-all answer to this question.

Consider a stock that has risen from 100 to 160 and has then fallen back to 150 to stop me out for a 50% profit. Would I re-establish my position at a price of 148.5 for a 1% discount? No way. What about a price of 135 for a 10% discount? Maybe, but it depends on the chart. Would I go in again at my original purchase price of 100 at a 33% discount? Almost certainly!

The point about this example is that *having banked a 50% profit* I would not want to hand much of it back by chasing the back stock down to my original purchase price. Except that if a £3-per-point pyramided position had stopped out, and if the chart was favourable, I might be tempted to establish a new smaller £1-per-point position for as little as the 1% discount – just in case I had been needlessly shaken out.

Automated Position Entry

My preference is to open positions *manually*, and close them *automatically*. I have the luxury of being able to do this because *this is my day job*.

Those of you who are trying to hold down another 'day job' will not be able to open new positions manually unless you have a very understanding employer or you trade on non-domestic markets: for example UK traders opening positions on American stocks after work.

If you find yourself in this position, it may be useful – indeed necessary – to utilise *limit orders* and *contingent stop orders* for automated entry.

Limit Orders for Automated Entry

If you think that a particular stock may become attractive as a position trade, because (for example) its price is historically very low on a long-term chart, you could place a *limit order* with your stockbroker or spread betting firm so as to establish a position for you automatically – when you're not watching – if the price falls further to a level you set.

For example: having noted that the Bloomsbury share price (see *Figure 15 Bloomsbury 5 Year Chart*) had bottomed out at about 110p a couple of times in 2008 and 2009, in January 2010 one might have placed a *limit order* to purchase this stock automatically if the price ever fell to 115p (just above the support level) on the basis that it would likely rebound. Such an order could have been placed at the time of your monthly or weekly portfolio review, and left to run for 30 days or *good till cancelled*.

A 'limit order to buy' is an order for your broker to buy shares when the price falls to the level you set, whereas a 'stop order to buy' would be an order to buy shares when the price rises to a level you set.

Now let's suppose you are in a position to review your portfolio each day, out of hours, but not in a position to place trades during trading hours. If during February 2010 you were expecting Shanks Group to make an announcement sometime soon regarding a potential takeover, which would have the potential to send the share price gap-down, but you did not know when the announcement will be made, then you could each evening place or revise a *limit order* to buy shares automatically the next day *if* the price gapped down substantially from the current price. For example: having noted a share price of 120p on the evening of 7 March (see *Figure 18 Shanks Group 9 March Price Gap Down*) you might have placed a *limit order* representing your desire to purchase shares if, and only if, the price gapped down by 20% to a price of 96p. Not that you knew anything about 7 March being the right time to place this order; since you would have placed a similar order previously on the evenings of 6 March and 5 March... and so on.

I have chosen this example because it was bound to work in retrospect, but I'm sure you get the general idea. And I note that the same approach could have worked on Prudential Corp, as shown in *Figure 17 Prudential 2 March Price Gap Down*.

Another source of candidate stocks on which to place such speculative limit orders would be your *Sold List* of previously stopped-out stocks.

Contingent Stop Orders

The problem with placing speculative limit orders that will execute automatically when you are not present is that the price may go on falling. When establishing positions manually I almost always attach a protective 'stop order to sell' slightly below my buy-in price, to guard against the possibility that *I was wrong* to buy in.

A 'stop order to sell' is an order for your broker to sell shares when the price falls to the level you set.

On some trading platforms it is possible to do something similar automatically by placing a *contingent order*. When placing the *limit order to buy*, you would state that *if done* (i.e. if the limit order executes) then a second order should be placed automatically to stop you out if the price falls further. This *limit order with a contingent stop order* would read something like this:

Place a limit order to buy if the price falls to 96p and (if done) place a stop order to sell at 89p.

A 'stop order to buy' is an order for your broker to BUY shares when the price falls to the level you specify, and a 'stop order to sell' is an order for your broker to SELL shares when the price falls to an even lower level that you specify.

Not all trading platforms provide this facility. And where they don't, you can still be reassured by the fact that your initial exploratory position should in any case be of a *small position size*.

Why I Prefer Manual Position Entry

Having just told you how you can place advance orders to enter trades automatically when you're not looking, I should tell you why i prefer not to.

It's bad enough to suffer the occasional price gap, spike, or slippage when closing a trade using a stop order, without having to suffer this on the way in to a trade too. Whereas on some platforms we can guarantee our stop-out price, we cannot usually guarantee our entry price.

When the price of Mouchel Group gapped-up on takeover rumours at the market open on 6 December (see *Figure 19 Mouchel Group Price Gap Up*) one of my blog followers reported that his opening order at 57p was filled by the broker immediately at the higher price of 73p.

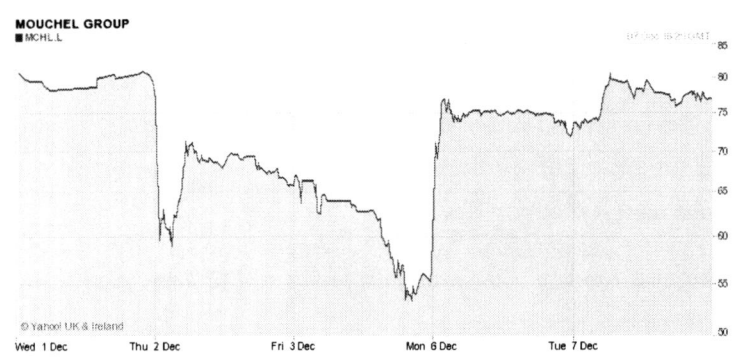

Figure 19 Mouchel Group Price Gap Up

Market Timing

By picking beaten-down stocks, and trading predominantly if not exclusively long only, you might think that I am predicting a recovery. While I don't agree with those commentators who say that it is impossible to time the markets, I'm not actually practicing pure market timing here. At any given time I have no idea whether the markets will recover or not, but I hope that my stock picks will outperform the markets if they do recover.

Suppose the markets rewound to their high points 2007, in which case (at the time of writing) the FTSE All Share index would recover by a mere 17% as shown in *Figure 20 FTSE All Share Index 2010-10-20*. If my stock picks also recovered their former glories they would become multi-baggers rather than 17% risers.

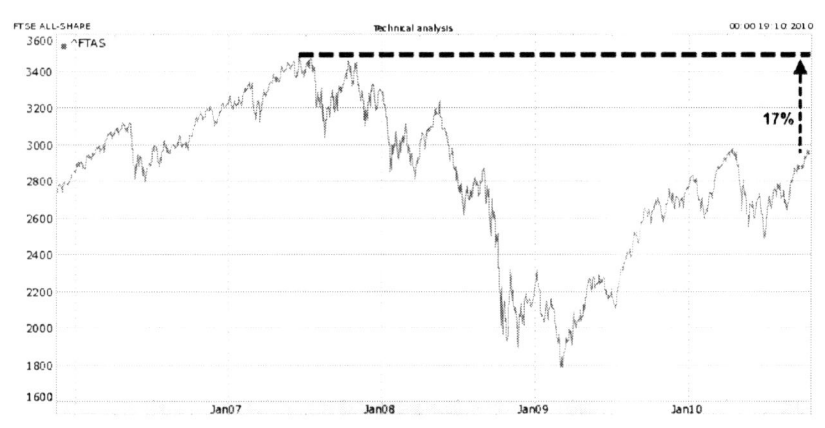

Figure 20 FTSE All Share Index 2010-10-20

Not (Quite) Trend Following

My Position Trading strategy is a trend-following strategy to the extent that I will hold a position for as long as it is trending upwards. But I don't wait for a trend to develop before jumping on board, instead preferring to catch a falling knife (which I know some people don't like). The following trade illustrates why I prefer to pre-empt a new trend.

Figure 21 Irish Life Daily Chart to mid-November 2010 shows that after a big drop at the end of October and into November, by mid-November it looked like Irish Life and Permanent had embarked on a new up-trend.

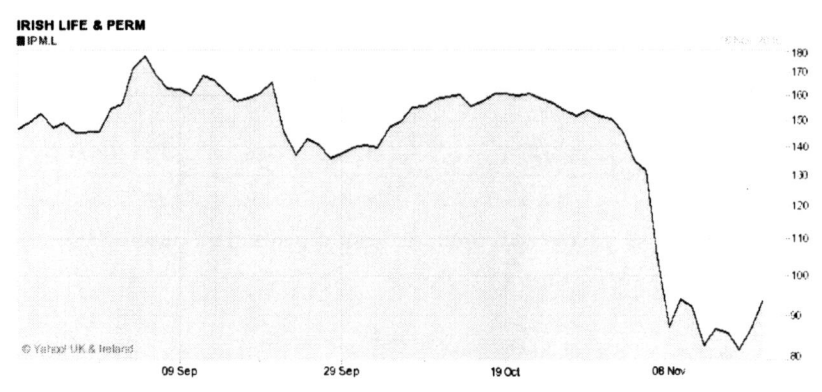

Figure 21 Irish Life Daily Chart to mid-November 2010

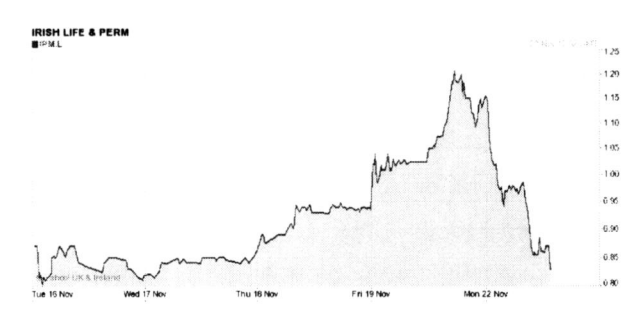

Figure 22 Irish Life 5-Minute Chart to 22 November 2010 shows what happened next. As soon as a trader could be sure that a new up-trend was under way, prompting him to buy, the trend abruptly reversed. With an initial stop order presumably somewhere in the 70s, the trader who bought into this 'established' up-trend could be nursing an initial loss of up to 35% in traditional investment terms or up to £40 at my £1-per-point default position size.

Figure 22 Irish Life 5-Minute Chart to 22 November 2010

By catching the falling knife at 90 instead, *I* went into profit almost immediately and ultimately banked a profit of £10 by stopping out at 100 when the false up-trend reversed. It may be nothing to shout about, but is much better than the *initial loss* suffered by the orthodox trend follower.

Some orthodox trend followers would argue that they would not identify an embryonic new up-trend *Figure 21* in the first place, because it did not yet meet their criteria for a series of higher highs and high lows or some combination of moving averages. The danger here is that the price will have risen even further from the price trough before a convincing up-trend could be identified.

If you think I'm implying that I would never buy into an established up-trend, I need to set you straight. The subtlety here is that actually I *would buy into an established up-trend*, providing *I could do so on a dip*. Just like the trend followers. And I would certainly *pyramid* into an established up-trend, as long as I could do so safely.

Stock Picking in a Nutshell

In a nutshell, my stock picking regime can be summarised as follows.

Establish an exploratory position with a small position size when a stock is priced historically (and possibly absolutely) very low, and when it has just undergone a significant price correction. When re-establishing a position, always do so at a price lower than your last stop-out price.

That's really all there is to it.

Incorporating Your Own Criteria

While I'm personally not a fundamentals-driven investor, those of you who are fundamentalists will note that the synopsis of my stock picking regime is actually not that inconsistent with your approach.

I think we can agree on purchasing stocks that are *"priced historically (and possibly absolutely) very low"* however we choose to judge them to be underpriced. I'm merely suggesting that we do so with a small initial position size – in case we are wrong, or in case we are right but *Mr. Market* does not yet realise we are right.

And while we may well disagree about buying on a significant correction, I see no logical reason why a fundamental investor would not wish to buy an undervalued stock when it is temporarily *even better value*.

I know that some experienced chartists will regard my stock picking regime as rather simplistic. I take this approach in part because I believe in it, and in part because in this book I wanted to concentrate on issues of money- and risk- management rather than attempting to daze and confuse you with a plethora of technical indicators.

The good news is that there is nothing to stop you enhancing (if you think you can) my overall strategy by incorporating your chart pattern spotting or other stock picking regime. I know that one of my blog followers did reasonably well in 2010 by betting on stock tips – yes, really – while using similar money- and risk- management techniques to me. Another blog follower runs positions in a very similar way to me, after first establishing those positions when he identifies significant areas of supply and demand imbalance on a price chart. And he's also rather fond of going short.

My point is that you can take my position trading approach as a complete but non-guaranteed trading system, or you can treat it merely as the starting point for your own trading strategy.

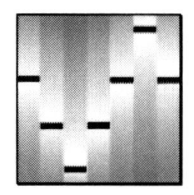

8 – On Dividends

Since the *position trading* approach encourages us to hold on to a rising stock for as long as possible – but not longer – there is a good chance of collecting dividends along the way; just like as an investor.

But unlike an investor, I see dividends as a useful bonus rather than as a reason for holding a stock. I aim to establish positions at what I think are attractive prices regardless of whether the stocks underpinning those positions have high or low dividend yields.

Dividend Yield is calculated as the annual dividend payment divided into the stock price. A stock priced at 100p that pays an annual dividend of 5p has a dividend yield of 5%; and investors would typically compare this rate-of-return with the rate that they would otherwise enjoy by placing their investment cash on deposit with a bank.

While I don't chase dividend yields, and I think it can be dangerous to do so, the receipt of dividends on long-held position can have some beneficial side effects.

Benefits of Dividends

The receipt of dividends allows you to:

- Take some reward for holding a position, by having some of your investment cash returned without having to *sell out* prematurely.

- Provide funds for pyramiding into *the best stock*, which might not be the same stock.

- Offset trading account fees, and financing charges on leveraged positions.

The first point is obvious, and to some extent more of a feel-good factor than anything else. The second point about *pyramiding* was covered in *Chapter 5 – On Pyramiding*. The third point deserves some further explanation.

Offsetting Account Fees with Dividends

Share trading is generally not free. Regular brokerage accounts and CFD accounts charge *transaction fees* on share purchases and sales, some tax-friendly accounts (such as Individual Savings Accounts and Self Invested Personal Pension accounts in the UK) charge additional *administration fees*, and even the government may levy additional fees in the form of stamp duty tax.

Even in the case of spread betting where you incur no direct fees; if you establish potentially long term positions as daily rolling spread bets, which I do, then you pay a daily financing rolling charge each day in order to keep the position open.

So while I do not invest for the *dividend income* itself, I do regard the receipt of dividends on some of my positions as going some way towards offsetting these various accounts fees while I hold my positions in anticipation of *capital appreciation*.

In a nutshell: if it costs me 5% of my investment to establish a single position and hold it for a year, and the stock in question pays a 5% dividend, then effectively it costs me nothing to hold that position. This is rather like the scenario in which you purchase a house with a mortgage, rent out the house to cover the mortgage payments, and you (not the tenant) benefit from any subsequent increase in the value of the house.

Dividends on Spread Bets

While on the subject of spread bets, you will know by now that I use these as my preferred (but not exclusive) trading vehicle. Those of you familiar with the receipt of dividends on traditional equity holdings and unfamiliar with spread bets may wonder if dividends are received on spread bets.

Spread bettors receive dividends on their long rolling positions, just as investors would, albeit perhaps by a slightly different mechanism: the spread betting company may close your position at one price and then re-open it at an adjusted price so that you benefit from the amount of the dividend. Or they may simply credit the amount of the dividend to your ledger balance. Either way, you are getting the dividend.

Note that short spread bet positions oblige you to 'pay the dividend' for the benefit of those holding long positions. Your short position will be adjusted automatically by the spread betting company to reflect this.

Concrete Examples of Offsetting Fees with Dividends

On 23 March 2010 I received a £15 dividend adjustment in relation to my long £1-per-point spread bet position in Aviva; this amount being sufficient to offset 75 days worth of rolling charges at £0.20-per-day on this position. Assuming an additional half-year dividend of half as much again, the total annual dividend receipts of £22.50 would offset 30% of the rolling charges for the year.

If anything, this represents a worst-case scenario because this particular spread betting firm applied higher-than-average rolling charges in exchange for free guaranteed stops. An Aviva position in a different spread betting account could have cost only £0.03-per-day in rolling charges, thus the £15 dividend would have been sufficient to offset 500 days worth of rolling charges!

Don't forget that the value of my Aviva holding will have fallen by the same £15 when the dividend adjustment was made, which is one of the reasons why I don't get too excited about dividends, but the dividend receipts do provide some help with rolling charges without requiring me meet those financing charges by closing existing positions.

On an equivalent-size traditional investment in a regular brokerage account there would be no rolling charges, but a £22.50 dividend receipt should at least offset the costs of buying and then selling the stock within the year. Any surplus dividends could by pyramided into existing or new positions as described in *Chapter 5 – On Pyramiding*.

Note also that on a traditional investment via a brokerage, the value of your investment would fall in line with the dividend payment on the *ex-dividend date*, but you would not actually receive the dividend until the *payment date*; whereas on a rolling spread bet you effectively receive the dividend on the earlier *ex-dividend date*.

Another example of offsetting rolling charges with dividends was illustrated by my blog posting of 22 September 2010 in which I reported that:

Goals Soccer Centres paid me a dividend of +£0.64 and had taken about £0.16 in overnight financing charges while accumulating a £22 profit of which £13.80 was locked in by my stop order. In a nutshell: it cost me just £0.16 to achieve a total *paper* profit of £22.64 and to secure (assuming no slippage) a total profit (including the dividend) of £14.44.

This was a good example of how my position trading strategy should work!

Why not look for High Yield?

Given what I said about using dividends to fully or at least partially offset the costs of holding a position, you may wonder why I do not therefore seek out high yielding stocks. I can think of three reasons why not:

First: I'm looking primarily for price appreciation, and steady dividend paying stocks tend to be mature stocks with little or no growth potential.

Second: Dividends can work against capital appreciation, to the extent that a stock that declares a 10% dividend will typically fall in price by 10% on the ex-dividend date to reflect the fact that new investors will not be entitled to the dividend.

Third: I proved to my own satisfaction in my book *"Stock Fundamentals On Trial: Do Dividend Yield, P/E, and PEG Really Work?"* that dividend yield is not a good predictor of future share price appreciation, and can in fact be a dangerous indicator. In 2007 many decades-old and even centuries-old financial firms showed very attractive dividend yields of more than 10% merely as a result of their plummeting share prices – remember that dividend yield is the dividend divided by the share price – and they promptly cut those dividends; or went bust.

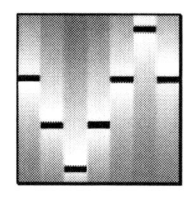

9 – Synthesis

Having covered the essential concepts that underpin my interpretation of the position trading strategy, in this chapter I explore the interrelationships between those concepts. In other words, how do the concepts fit together into an over-arching *position trading system*?

The Seven Pillars of Position Trading

A successful *position trading system* rests on seven pillars – Diversification, Stop Orders, Position Sizing, Pyramiding, Leverage, Stock Picking, and Dividends – as outlined in the prior seven chapters, and as shown in *Figure 23 The Seven Pillars of Position Trading*.

Figure 23 The Seven Pillars of Position Trading

Diversification allows us to *spread our risk* across positions and over time.

Stop Orders allow us to *cut our losses,* and *lock-in our profits* without crystallising them prematurely.

Position Sizing ensures that we do *not risk too much money too soon.*

Pyramiding means that we back the winners.

Leverage amplifies our gains (and losses, so be careful).

Stock Picking helps us to establish the right positions at the right time.

Dividends help to offset the costs of holding our positions, and provide a source of fund for pyramiding.

Daily Routine

On a daily basis, but sometimes less frequently and often more frequently, I cycle through the daily routine shown in *Figure 24 Daily Routine.*

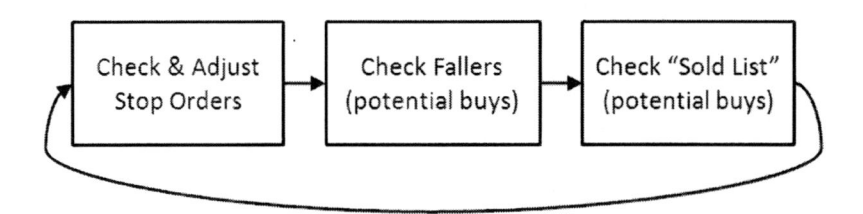

```
┌──────────────────┐    ┌──────────────────┐    ┌──────────────────┐
│  Check & Adjust  │ →  │  Check Fallers   │ →  │ Check "Sold List"│
│   Stop Orders    │    │ (potential buys) │    │ (potential buys) │
└──────────────────┘    └──────────────────┘    └──────────────────┘
         ↑_____|
```

Figure 24 Daily Routine

I describe each of the three boxes in the three subsections that follow.

Check & Adjust Stop Orders

I regard my approach as working when I spend more time maintaining my existing positions than I spend establishing new

POSITION TRADING

positions. And I maintain those positions by manually trailing my stop orders: by adjusting my stop levels upwards – never down, on a long position – so as to reduce my risk or lock-in some profit.

Thus the first thing I do each day, or sometimes each hour, and at least each week, is to check the stop levels on all of my current positions. How frequently can sometimes be dependent on my own personal boredom level (it's better for me to relieve this boredom by adjusting stops orders than by establishing new positions) and dependent on what the markets as a whole are doing. When markets are shooting upwards there may be a lot of scope for upwards adjustments, and when markets are tanking there may be no point in looking.

As a shortcut when I don't have time to check every one of my positions, I will sometimes refer to the *Yahoo! Finance Price % Winners* lists as a source of candidates for raising stop orders:

FTSE All Share Price % Winners at http://uk.finance.yahoo.com/gainers?e=ftas

NYSE Price % Winners at http://uk.finance.yahoo.com/gainers?e=nq

NASDAQ Price % Winners at http://uk.finance.yahoo.com/gainers?e=o

EuroStoxx 50 Price % Winners at http://uk.finance.yahoo.com/gainers?e=stoxx50e

If I recognize one of the day's big winners as one of my holdings, I'll take a look at its stop level.

> 2nd Edition Note: I now use the Position Trading Cockpit spreadsheet discussed in *Chapter 11 – Automating the Strategy* instead.

I like to trail my stops on long term positions no closer than 15% below the current market price. So if I find that a stop is wider than this, I will adjust it upwards – but with the level tweaked slightly to ensure that the stop can remain below any significant support price.

See *Appendix A – Support and Resistance* for more information on support prices.

When first establishing a position I will usually apply a very tight stop initially, and thereafter I will typically let the stop distance widen to the 15%-20% range before adjusting it at all. The exception to this rule is where my trading platform imposes a minimum initial stop distance, in which case I would need to raise my stop level aggressively as soon as possible simply for it to reach the level I intended at the outset.

Check for Pyramiding Opportunities
This check perhaps does not deserve an item of its own, but when assessing stop levels against current prices it may be useful to note those stocks that are close to stopping out. As long as there is sufficient locked-in profit to justify an additional position, pyramiding into a position that is likely to stop out is a *low risk* time to pyramid because the stop order on the new position can be set *very tight*.

Check Fallers (potential buys)

Whereas rocketing markets are my cue to concentrate on *Check & Adjust Stop Orders*, falling markets are my cue to *Check Fallers (potential buys)*. Take note, though, that you never know what individual big fallers you will find even when the overall tide is rising.

I will typically find candidate stocks by referring to the *Yahoo! Finance Price % Losers* lists:

FTSE All Share Price % Losers at http://uk.finance.yahoo.com/losers?e=ftas

NYSE Price % Losers at http://uk.finance.yahoo.com/losers?e=nq

NASDAQ Price % Losers at http://uk.finance.yahoo.com/losers?e=o

EuroStoxx 50 Price % Losers at http://uk.finance.yahoo.com/losers?e=stoxx50e

POSITION TRADING

What percentage must they fall? There is no perfect answer to this question, but in general the bigger fallers (bottom of the list) are the better candidates. After identifying a candidate, I will then look at its chart. What I'm looking for is ideally a gapped-down price on a stock that is also down to a historic low.

> 2nd Edition Note: I now use the Position Trading Cockpit spreadsheet discussed in *Chapter 11 – Automating the Strategy* instead.

Check "Stop-Out List" (potential re-entries)

When a position stops out, I place the stock on my *Stop-Out List* which is a kind of watch-list detailing the price at which I last exited each stock. Remember from *Chapter 7 – On Stock Picking* that in the absence of other compelling reasons to repurchase a stock, I will do so only if I can secure a lower purchase price than my last selling price; the lower, the better.

When position-trading short (betting on falling prices) I might utilise the opposite notion of re-selling at a higher price those stocks that I had previously exited at a lower price with a 'stop order to buy'.

It used to be the case that the *Stop-Out List* required some periodic maintenance to remove those stocks whose prices have moved so far from my last stop-out price that there was no near-term prospect of re-establishing a position at a more favourable price. Also, some stocks would not make it onto my *Stop-Out List* in the first place if I considered them to be overvalued when they last stopped out. The requirement to keep my *Stop-Out List manageable* has been removed thanks to automating my *Stop-Out List* using the *Position Trading Cockpit* spreadsheet.

I can now easily monitor all of the FTSE All Share stocks (for example), and my ideal would be to reach the point at which every single stock is either in my live portfolio (so it's making a profit) or is on my *Stop-Out List* (so I know when to re-purchase it at a discount).

When to Sell

You will notice that in my daily routine there are no boxes marked *Check for Stocks to Sell* or *Check for Positions to Close*. That's because I hardly ever choose to manually sell a stock and close a position; my stop orders do that for me – automatically. I let the market decide when my positions should be closed.

Very occasionally I might make a conscious decision to sell because of some combination of:

- I am partially closing a profit; e.g. closing £1-per-point of a £2-per-point position, or closing £1000 of a £2000 position.

- I need to free up funds for a compelling opportunity at a time when I am fully invested and have no powder dry.

- I think the market as a whole is overheated, and I would like to put some cash on the sidelines in anticipation of a future correction.

- A single equity has enjoyed a sudden, significant rise, a price spike or 'gap up' that is likely to reverse.

Note that these are exceptions that prove (i.e. test) the rule, rather than the rule itself. The rule is to let the market decide when a position should be closed.

In fact, I might be just as likely to simply tighten my stop under these conditions so as to stop-out at the first sign of trouble without crystallising my profit prematurely by manually closing a position.

Other People's Money

You will see in *Chapter 10 – Proof of the Pudding* that I have on more than one occasion cashed-out completely at exactly the right time. It shows that market timing is possible, but it isn't easy, and in the second case I failed to time my overall re-entry correctly. One of my blog followers and reviewer of the first edition of this book suggested the inclusion of some tips on when to cash out completely by determining that a bull run had ended.

I'm not sure it's possible to identify market tops and bottoms accurately, and by cashing out completely you run the risk of having cashed out too soon during a sustained trend. What interests me more is deciding when to take back my original 'stake' or 'investment' so as to continue playing with profits that I have accumulated; i.e. playing with *other people's money*.

In the first publicly documented trading run outlined in *Chapter 10 – Proof of the Pudding* I accumulated some £18,000 from initial stakes totalling just £600. What is most important is not the fact that I cashed-out at the right time – which may be more luck than judgment – but the fact that in the second public run (the Trading Trail 2010) I committed only £1000 and later increased it to total funding of £1500 when conditions proved difficult. So while at the lowest point I had lost some £800 during the second run, this was £800 of *other people's money* and a mere fraction of my previous 'winnings'.

The point I'm making here is that when your £1000 portfolio becomes £2000, it may be prudent to take your original £1000 deposit off the table and continue playing only with *other people's money*.

Some authors suggest that maxing out on margin on leveraged trades is an effective way of speculating with *other people's money*. For a deposit of only £1000 you can control assets worth £10,000 thanks to the *other people's money* you have borrowed. But beware that you can still be on the line for the full amount, and the *other people's money* soon becomes *your money* when you face a margin call. It's rather like buying a £100,000 house using a £10,000 deposit and a £90,000 mortgage, and then finding yourself having to find the entire amount when the house burns down and you forgot to insure it.

Not the Buying or Selling, but the Waiting

There will be times, when the markets are moving sideways, that there is really not much to do. With the markets not going down there will be fewer bargain basement bargains to be had; and with the markets not going up there will be fewer opportunities to ratchet up stop orders and lock in profits.

What you should do in this situation is… nothing!

You don't have to trade every day, and sometimes – as legendary traders such as Jesse Livermore have gone on record as commenting – the big money is made by *waiting* for the right opportunity to come along.

In this respect the non-professional trader or investor may have an advantage over the professionals. You don't need to 'do something' in order to justify your salary as a trader; and you are under no pressure from your customers to 'stay invested' or to follow the latest investment fad.

I found to my cost that daily blogging a trading account <u>did</u> put me under this pressure, even though I had no investors to placate.

On Drawing Down and Staying Solvent

As King Canute discovered, we can't turn back the tide and make the markets go the way we want. We may not even be able to predict which way the tide will go, though we try. So we can't affect the unfolding market conditions, and maybe not predict those conditions, but what we can do is to make more money when conditions are favourable (for our strategy) than we lose when conditions are unfavourable.

What I am saying is that we cannot avoid draw-downs, those periods – sometimes prolonged – during which we lose money and our portfolio value goes down. You'll see some good real-life examples in *Chapter 10 – Proof of the Pudding*.

The problem with draw-downs is that if you lose 50% of your funds, you have to make a 100% profit in order to recover. It's possible to make the 100% recovery profit with this strategy, but that doesn't necessarily mean it is *likely*. And the last thing you want is for a big draw-down to wipe you out before you get to make the big profit that is just around the corner.

My first suggestion is: start small. If you have £10,000 available for spread betting, risk only £1000 of it initially. So what if you lose 50%? The £500 loss is only 5% of your total funds, and you have plenty of funds left with which to *play again*.

My second suggestion is: take money off the table. If your £1000 risk capital becomes £2000, why care if you then draw-down 50% of your 'profit' as long as you have taken your original £1000 off the table?

I've heard all the sage advice about always *playing for meaningful stakes*, and I understand that if you start with £500 and double your money then, well, you're still poor. But in this strategy I aim to multi-bag my money (e.g. from £500 to £5000) when the time is right, so there is really no pressure to *play for meaningful stakes* at the risk of not *staying in the game*.

Remember that the best golfers are not the ones who hit the biggest shots but the ones who make fewest mistakes. As far as I know, it's the same with professional poker players. In a world where the markets can stay irrational longer than we can stay solvent, we must strive above all to remain solvent while the markets remain irrational.

Dealing with Mistakes

While on the subject of mistakes it is worth saying something about what we should do when we make them – as we surely will. By mistakes, I don't mean trades that exit at a loss. I mean those things that were summarised so expertly by one of my blog readers:

"I have done £50 a point instead of 50p a point, I have doubled positions instead of closing them, I have forgotten to close stop orders on where they are not linked to open positions, I have bought the wrong instrument, I have gone long instead of short and vice versa, I have closed positions for the wrong amount and left a residual bet in play, and I have set stop loss orders for the wrong amount."

So, what should we do when we make these mistakes? Answer: rectify them immediately at the cost of hopefully just the spread. Don't wait for the mistake to rectify itself. Don't hope that the price will fall on your unintentional short position or that your unintentional £50-per-point position will make you an accidental millionaire.

What about Short Position Trading?

The position trading approach described in this book assumes a long trading stance. Positions are established by buying at low prices and then selling eventually at high prices, usually by stopping out.

This is the motivation behind the *Trailing Stop Buy, Trailing Stop Sell* trading pattern documented in my book "Financial Trading Patterns".

POSITION TRADING

Theoretically the same strategy could be executed in reverse by first selling at what is a high price, then by pyramiding additional funds as the share price continues to fall, and ultimately by selling out at a low price by being stopped out.

I do this occasionally; but not often because of the following reasons:

- Short trading can only be done in certain kinds of trading accounts, such as spread betting or CFD accounts, and not usually in regular brokerage (including tax friendly) accounts.

- Whereas in long trading the upside is potentially infinite and the downside finite (because shares don't fall below zero), in short trading the downside is potentially infinite (as share prices can theoretically rise forever) and the upside is finite (if the company goes bust). So it is even more important to mitigate the downside risk through the effective use of stop orders, and it is not possible to run our profits forever.

- In the long run, so far at least, stock markets always rise.

- Since position trading has much in common with investing, it may feel somewhat unnatural to bet on company failures.

With those caveats in mind, there is no reason to suppose that the position trading approach cannot be adapted to short trading.

Long Trades can benefit from Falling Prices

Traders place short trades in order to benefit from falling prices. When running the position trading strategy long-only you can also benefit from falling prices as I'll now explain.

Suppose you start with £1000 trading resources.

You establish a long position with a stop-loss order that gives you a risk of £100 (which is too high, but it helps with the illustration). When the price falls, and your position stops out, your resources fall to £900. You wait for the price to fall as far again, and you buy again, thus avoiding the additional £100 loss that you would have suffered if you had simply held. You latest '£100 risk' stop order means that when the price falls again, you lose another £100 taking your resources to £800. Once again, you sit out the next £100 fall. And repeat, until the price bottoms-out and you have taken a total £400 loss out of the possible £800 loss.

On the way back up to the starting price your latest position generates the full £800 gross 'recovery' profit, of which half is real net profit due to your avoided losses on the way down. It's shown pictorially in *Figure 25 Benefit from Falling* Prices.

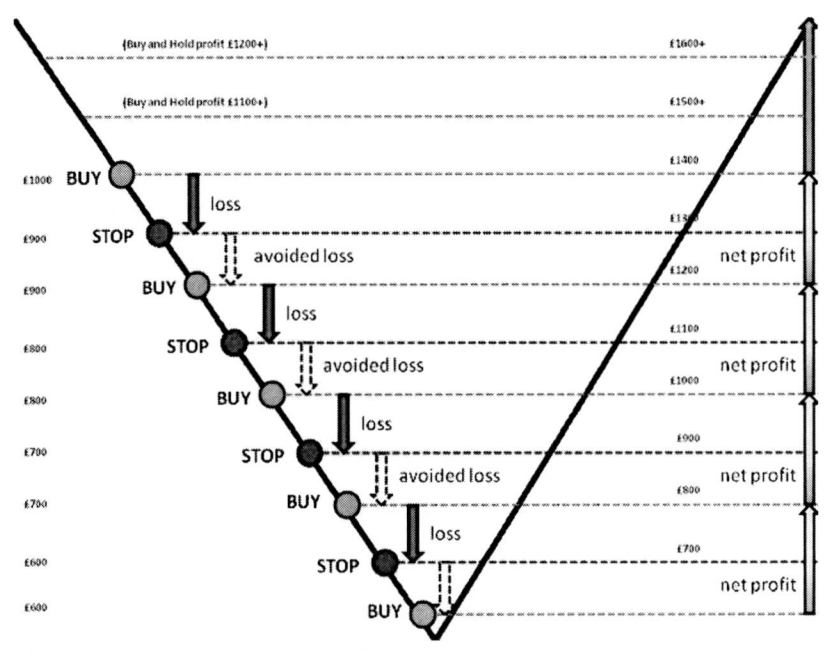

Figure 25 Benefit from Falling Prices

POSITION TRADING

The bottom line is that you end up with £1400 compared with £1000 for the buy-and-holder who simply held all the way down and all the way back up. Just like the buy-and-holder, you will make yet more profit – but will always be £400 ahead – as the price goes on rising above the original price. The buy-and-holder would have drawn down to as low as £200 along the way compared with your £600 minimum retained trading funds. Another trader who 'averaged down' would have gone bust in search of an even greater recovery profit.

This example shows that benefitting from falling prices as a long position trader is *possible*; but whether or not it is *probable* (i.e. likely) depends on your skill. In this idealised scenario the price eventually recovered, and we managed to establish our final position at or near the bottom of the cycle.

In reality you would not catch the exact bottom, and you wouldn't need to. You would not put all your eggs in one basket on the assumption that a single stock would surely recover, and you wouldn't go risking £100-a-time in a £1000 account. Would you?

Putting this into the context of the overall position trading strategy, you would not even begin this process unless a stock had already fallen a long way – so that the potential upside above the original price was much larger than the potential downside below the original price. And once the price had recovered to its starting point – if not before – you might pyramid the position in order to realise even greater gains on the way up.

The Three Phases of Position Trading

As the wider markets cycle through bull and bear phases the position trading strategy cycles through three phases:

#1 The Bear Phase: during which stocks are falling and the challenge is to catch as many falling (ideally fallen) knives as possible using a small stake... and while staying solvent.

#2 The Bull Phase: during which stocks are rising and accrued profits, locked in using stop orders, can be recycled as additional pyramided positions; the challenge being to pyramid rapidly enough to amplify profits without risking all of those profits.

#3 The Turning Phase: which marks the return from bull trend to bear trend, and at which time the challenge would ideally be to cash out completely... and then wait.

These three phases are driven to some extent by the overall market cycles. A rising tide lifts all boats, and vice versa. However, each individual position has its own lifecycle and once a sufficiently diverse set of positions have been established you may well see some positions in their bull phases while others are in their bear phases.

Effect of Interest Rates

I'm not going to share any words of wisdom about the relationship between central bank interest rates, bond yields, and stock prices. I'm not an economist, and I don't need to be.

I'd just like to make the point that this position trading strategy works best in times of low interest rates (so that overnight financing charges are low) and low stock prices (so there is plenty of upside potential to more-than counteract those low financing charges). Such conditions existed in 2008, 2009, and 2010.

Earlier in the same decade, up to 2007, interest rates were considerably higher – not on a historic scale, but compared with the subsequent years – and stock prices were also at a peak. With higher interest rates (hence higher financing charges) combined with higher stock prices (hence lower prospects for capital appreciation), this approach may not have been so effective.

At such times it may be prudent to consider short position trading. In a spread betting account (in particular) you will usually *receive* overnight financing charges for holding short positions, and obviously it is better to receive such income when interest rates are high. And with stock prices also high, you may anticipate more downside potential than upside potential in capital terms. With the benefit of hindsight, the year 2007 was a good year to 'go short'.

This is an idea, not a recommendation, and I do not *yet* have any concrete proof (see *chapter 10 – Proof of the Pudding*) that it will work as effectively purely on the short side.

What about Other Financial Instruments?

The position trading approach described in this book assumes that we will trade individual stocks rather than indices, commodities, or currencies.

I focus on stocks because:

- I am more familiar with stock markets than I am with commodity or currency markets, and I have proven to my own satisfaction that this approach works with individual equities.

- There are more individual equities to choose from than there are indices, commodities, or currency pairs; therefore more opportunities and more scope for diversification of holdings.

- Many stocks pay dividends, which helps to offset trading costs and rolling charges when positions are held indefinitely. *But the same is true of index positions.*

- Due to their low prices compared with some other financial instruments it is possible to establish individual stock positions with a *small initial position size* and / or with a *low initial risk*.

With those points in mind, there is no reason why the position trading approach cannot be adapted for index position trading, commodity position trading, or currency position trading. Most if not all trading decisions are made with respect to price action rather than fundamentals; so anything with a fluctuating (and ideally trending) price could be position-traded.

Position Trading for Fundamental Investors

Even if, as a fundamental investor, you purchase stocks when you think they have attractive price-earnings (P/E) ratios, or have good growth prospects reflected by their PEG, or because they are high yielders; and even if you choose to sell those stocks manually when their fundamentals are unattractive; you may yet find some value – no pun intended – in the money management regime I have documented in this book.

For example:

- Diversification *over time* as well as *across assets* will help you to spread your risk.

- The application of *stop orders* as an if-all-else-fails exit mechanism, a mere safety net, may be a useful complement to your preferred exit strategy; and will be especially useful when you're "not watching" the markets.

- A healthy attitude to *position sizing* will ensure that you don't bet the farm on any one position.

And I don't need to tell you about the value of collecting dividends.

If you're one of the Long Term Buy and Hold (LTBH) brigade, I may also have prompted you to consider not holding *unconditionally*. Unlike day trading, swing trading, and other short-to-medium term trading approaches, *position trading* could be construed as a perfectly valid *investment* strategy.

Remember that:

A long-term investment is a short-term [position] trade gone well!

Defensive Trading

In order to trade successfully over the long term we need to have *an edge* that gives the strategy a *positive expectancy*. A casino owner has a definite edge by virtue of the laws of physics and probability. The roulette wheel (for example) is biased in his favour such that he *knows for sure* that he will come out ahead of his customers over the long term.

Having an edge that gives a positive expectancy is necessary (else you can never come out ahead) but is not sufficient. Even the casino owner with his guaranteed edge must guard against any short-term shocks that may arise en route to realising his positive expectancy. His long-term edge is of no comfort when the first punter to walk through the door experiences enough "beginner's luck" to wipe out the casino's cash float. The casino must be sufficiently well capitalised and should have strategies for limiting its losses by restricting the size of bets that can be placed and (in extreme cases) by *stopping the game* or *throwing out the successful gambler*.

In a nutshell: the casino owner need not worry about the upside potential, which is guaranteed, as long as he manages the downside risk.

In this Position Trading strategy my philosophy is to play defensively by *taking care of the downside* and *letting the upside take care of itself*.

If I have an edge, then I need to stay in the game long enough to realise it. If I don't have an edge, then no amount of big bets on wild swings will save me... except by sheer luck.

Does it Really Work?

So much for the theory outlined in this book, but you may be left wondering "Does it really work?"

Do I really have an edge?

Unlike the casino owner, as traders we can never really be sure that we have an edge. No amount of back testing and no historic trail of good results can guarantee an edge that will continue into the future. But for as long as the juxtaposition of good and bad results outlined in the next chapter (and undocumented elsewhere) continues to play out in a similar way, I'll continue to work on the assumption that my Position Trading strategy has 'the edge'.

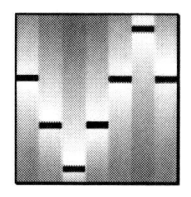

10 – Proof of the Pudding

Talk is cheap, and trading is expensive – if you get it wrong. So you would be justified in wondering: does the position trading approach outlined in this book really work?

Let me tell you about my own track record.

From Loser to Winner

I dabbled in trading in all its forms – regular brokerage, contracts for difference, spread betting, covered warrants – for several years part-time with no success. In fact I lost a lot of money; mainly because I could afford to. I'm no idiot, and I was clever enough follow the advice to "only invest what you can afford to lose". As a very successful IT consultant with a high income I could afford to lose a lot of money... so I did!

When I gave up the day job to become a writer, publisher, and more-or-less fulltime trader I couldn't afford to lose much money... so I didn't. And I made back what I had lost.

Having devised what appeared to be good strategy for making a lot of money (when it works) and not losing too much (when it doesn't) I set about documenting my evolution as a trader and the features of what has become my Position Trading approach.

I also started keeping better records and set about publishing warts 'n' all accounts of my real-life real-money portfolios that were being run along the principles outlined in this book.

3000% in Six Months (2009)

This real-life portfolio first featured in my book *"Stop Orders"* published by Harriman House (ISBN 1906659281). Rather than duplicate what I wrote before, I'll explain it here with new words and pictures.

The bottom line is that I grew an initial stake of only £300 to over £9000 – that's a more than 3000% increase – in a spread betting account between March and September 2009. Not only once, but twice, in two separate (but simultaneous) accounts, so that in total £600 became more than £18,000.

Figure 26 Equity Curve for 3000% in Six Months shows the equity curve for one of those accounts in the specified time period.

It may be worth noting that the FTSE 100 index appreciated by about 40% (compared with my 3000%) over the same period. So I beat the FTSE 100 index by a factor of 75!

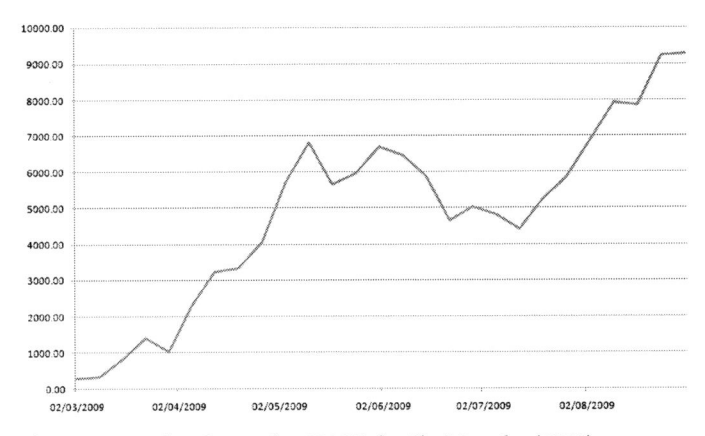

Figure 26 Equity Curve for 3000% in Six Months (2009)

If you're wondering why I ran a more-or-less identical portfolio in two separate accounts; it was in part because I was trialling two different spread betting firms, and in part because I like to spread my risk between accounts. I see two separate spread bets at £1-per-point (for example) in two separate accounts as less risky than a single £2-per-point spread bet in one account. I made this point in the *Diversification Across Platforms* section of *Chapter 2 – On Diversification*, where I also pointed out that this form of diversification is less desirable in brokerage accounts that encourage *larger investments* by imposing per-transaction dealing fees.

Trading Trail, January to April 2010

In 2010 I undertook a further public demonstration in the form of my *Trading Trail* blog (http://tradingtrail.blogspot.com) described as follows.

In January 2010 Tony Loton established a demonstration spread betting account with a starting capital of just £1000, with the aim of growing this to a sizeable sum (or at least not losing much money) by the end of the year. This blog documents the performance of the account, including the trades made with associated commentary, over the course of the year to December 2010.

I ran the near-real-time and real-money public *Trading Trail* account initially for four months, at which time I went fully to cash for a profit of just over 60% in that time as shown in *Figure 27 Trading Trail, January - April 2010*.

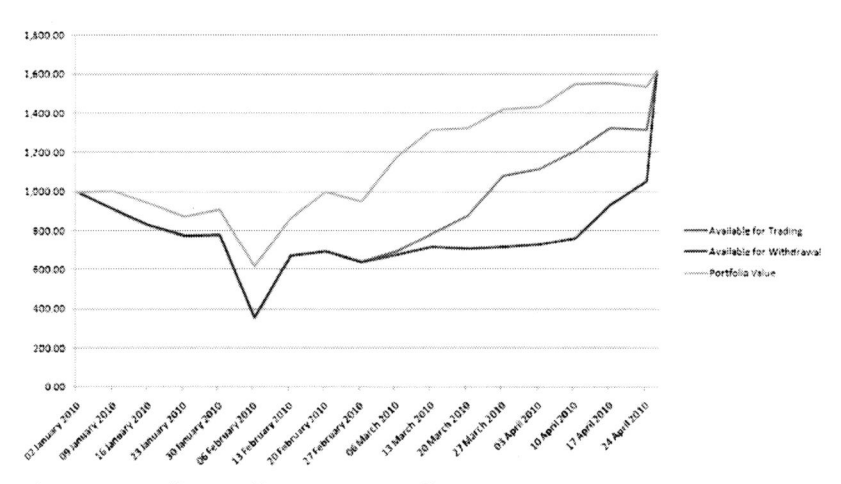

Figure 27 Trading Trail, January - April 2010

This result was achieved by following exactly the position trading techniques outlined in the previous chapters of this book. You can see from the chart that it wasn't all plain sailing. Capital draw-downs are inevitable, especially while establishing a foothold in the market, which is why the focus on money management was so important. We must live to trade another day.

In this case the draw-downs were actually made much worse by the fact that I undertook some madcap index day-trading early in the *Trading Trail*, simply to liven things up for my blog followers. This in itself demonstrates an important principle of trading, which is: once you have a system that works, stick with it and don't experiment with other approaches merely for the sake of it. For me, the 'system that works' is the position trading system described in this book.

From 27 February onwards you can see that as my total *Portfolio Value* increased, so did my *Available for Trading* figure (middle line). This was a direct consequence of me trailing my stop orders upwards so as to lock-in some of the accrued profit. It meant that from 27 March onwards my minimum worse-case-scenario value (if all my positions stopped out in some cataclysmic event) was greater than my starting capital. In other words, from this point onwards I could not lose any of my original capital.

Nurture and Prune

Do you remember what I told you in the opening chapter about nurturing and pruning our positions? This is illustrated by the two Trading Trail portfolio snapshots shown in *Figure 28 Trading Trail* Portfolio at 16 January 2010 and *Figure 29 Trading Trail* Portfolio at 27 March 2010.

Notice how the second portfolio contains more stock positions than the first portfolio, but with some of the initial stocks (e.g. Sports Direct) not present in the later snapshot. Notice also how the Citigroup position is dated differently in the second snapshot, reflecting the fact that the original position – established on 05 Jan – stopped out at a price of 340.50 and was re-purchased at a lower price of 317.40 on 27 Jan.

Date	Description	Stake	Open Price	Price To Close	Stop/Limit	P&L (If Closed)	Risk/GTD Profit
05Jan	Citigroup	1.00	348.50	340.50	309 /	-8.00	-39.50
06Jan	Inchcape	1.00	29.00	29.00	19.57 /	0.00	-9.43
06Jan	Game Group	1.00	107.20	100.10	95 /	-7.10	-12.20
07Jan	Yell Group	1.00	38.58	37.90	28.09 /	-0.68	-10.49
08Jan	HMV	1.00	92.60	80.30	76 /	-12.30	-16.60
11Jan	Redrow	1.00	139.40	136.00	109 /	-3.40	-30.40
12Jan	Debenhams	1.00	73.90	67.50	63.40 /	-6.40	-10.50
14Jan	Home Retail Group	1.00	271.50	259.80	257.16 /	-11.70	-14.34
14Jan	Premier Foods	1.00	36.10	32.88	25.88 /	-3.22	-10.22
14Jan	Sports Direct	1.00	95.20	97.30	84.10 /	2.10	-11.10

Figure 28 Trading Trail Portfolio at 16 January 2010

Date	Description	Stake	Open Price	Price To Close	Stop/Limit	P&L (If Closed)	Risk/GTD Profit
06Jan	Inchcape	1.00	29.00	29.25	20.46 /	0.25	-8.54
07Jan	Yell Group	1.00	38.58	40.68	33.28 /	2.10	-5.30
11Jan	Redrow	1.00	139.40	141.60	130.14 /	2.20	-9.26
14Jan	Premier Foods	1.00	36.10	32.70	25.92 /	-3.40	-10.18
27Jan	Citigroup	1.00	317.40	429.40	390.96 /	112.00	73.56
05Feb	ICAP	1.00	308.30	379.60	363.37 /	71.30	55.07
05Feb	HMV	1.00	75.10	86.80	77.70 /	11.70	2.60
05Feb	Qinetiq Group	1.00	126.50	134.70	127.71 /	8.20	1.21
05Feb	Rank Group	1.00	88.20	115.60	106.83 /	27.40	18.63
05Feb	Segro	1.00	305.00	324.50	310.84 /	19.50	5.84
05Feb	Barratt Developments	1.00	114.50	129.00	117.09 /	14.50	2.59
08Feb	Aviva	1.00	351.90	384.10	367.75 /	32.20	15.85
08Feb	KESA	1.00	119.80	127.80	115.38 /	8.00	-4.42
08Feb	Old Mutual	1.00	96.20	122.50	120.27 /	26.30	24.07
08Feb	National Express Group	1.00	198.30	228.90	206.10 /	30.60	7.80
09Feb	Aberdeen Asset Mngment	1.00	112.40	129.60	117.09 /	17.20	4.69
12Feb	Ashtead Group	1.00	77.00	96.80	88.20 /	19.80	11.20
12Feb	Game Group	1.00	84.80	102.80	93.30 /	18.00	8.50
12Feb	Royal Bank Of Scotland	1.00	31.19	45.54	40.70 /	14.35	9.51
25Feb	Hays	1.00	103.60	108.60	98.01 /	5.00	-5.59
25Feb	Enterprise Inns	1.00	101.70	133.20	119.52 /	31.50	17.82
25Feb	MAN Group	1.00	220.20	242.10	238.26 /	21.90	18.06
26Feb	Regus	1.00	83.30	117.90	108.20 /	34.60	24.90
02Mar	Prudential Corp	1.00	504.60	531.90	510.05 /	27.30	5.45
02Mar	Cookson Group	1.00	445.50	552.10	503.19 /	106.60	57.69

Figure 29 Trading Trail Portfolio at 27 March 2010

Notice that the holding periods for stocks still in the portfolio at the later date range from one month (Prudential Corp and Cookson Group, bought on 02 March) to three months (Inchcape, bought on 06 January). Individual positions may ultimately be held for much longer, even for years, or may be opened and then stopped out within a day.

In the later portfolio snapshot shown in *Figure 30 Trading Trail Portfolio (partial) at 24 November 2010* you can see that two of the positions – in Lavendon and Severfield-Rowen – have been pyramided up to £2-per-point and are showing healthy profits.

POSITION TRADING

Market/Trade	Opened	Size	Type	Stop	Limit	Margin	Level	Current		P/L (GBP)
Lavendon Rolling Daily	27/08/2010 08:17	2	Buy			40.20	57.3	78.1	▲	41.50
Minerva Rolling Daily	11/11/2010 13:20	1	Buy	68.0		19.88	75.2	72.4	▼	(2.80)
Party Gaming plc Rolling Daily	11/11/2010 12:22	1	Buy	223.0		11.94	209.0	237.3	▲	28.30
Punch Taverns Rolling Daily	19/11/2010 09:28	1	Buy	51.0		10.00	59.0	59.2	▲	0.20
Pv Crystalox Rolling Daily	04/11/2010 09:01	1	Buy	48.0		14.00	51.0	54.1	▲	3.10
Regal Petroleum Rolling Daily	10/11/2010 13:07	1	Buy	5.6		12.50	15.6	11.9	▼	(3.70)
Rentokil Rolling Daily	05/11/2010 14:53	1	Buy	85.5		12.50	95.5	90.6	▼	(4.90)
Royal Bank of Scotland Rolling Daily	23/11/2010 09:59	1	Buy	36.0		5.00	39.8	40.4	▲	0.60
Severfield-Rowen Rolling Daily	26/08/2010 08:18	2	Buy			130.20	220.9	256.9	▲	71.90

Figure 30 Trading Trail Portfolio (partial) at 24 November 2010

By presenting you with a partial portfolio snapshot from November 2010 I am getting somewhat ahead of myself, because first I need to tell you about...

Trading Trail, the Great Unravel

It turns out that I cashed in my chips at exactly the right time, almost to the day before the markets took a turn for the worse in April / May 2010. I cashed in so as to switch accounts to one that would be more suitable for the public experiment. In private I might have waited and watched for a while before planning my re-entries, but in public I felt pressured to keep my blog readers entertained lest they should drift away. That's where it all started to unravel as I re-established my old positions far too soon and was left with little choice but to follow the market lower and lower as shown in *Figure 31 Trading Trail, the Great Unravel*.

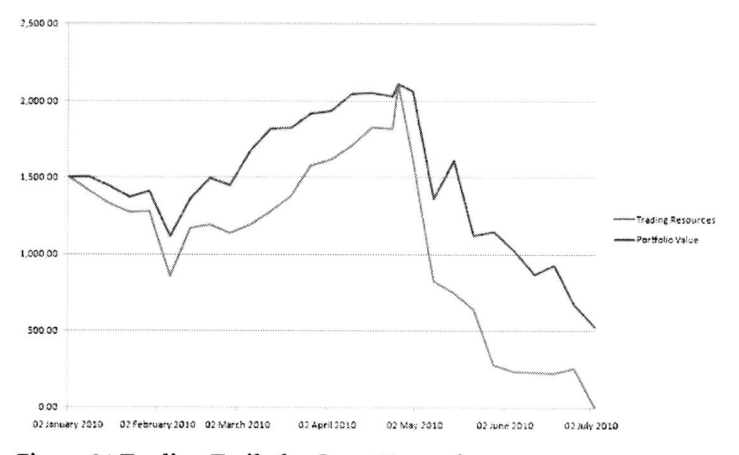

Figure 31 Trading Trail, the Great Unravel

This phase of the Trading Trail was all about *staying in the game* by not doing anything as stupid as 'averaging down' or doubling my stakes as my trading capital sank lower and lower. It has been said that the market can stay irrational longer than you can stay solvent, and my objective here was to stay solvent longer than the market could stay irrational. At this point it is worth remembering that I had drawn-down significantly before, yet recovered to ever higher levels.

On the way down I decided to re-capitalise the account with an additional £500, thereby re-stating the original budget as £1500. This was controversial, but necessary, and served to illustrate just how important it was to have committed a mere fraction of the previous year's gains in this year's public trading run.

If I could demonstrably make £18,000 in one year, and lose only £1000 (at the lowest point) of it the next year then I wouldn't be doing too bad; especially if it turned out alright in the end.

The Great Unravel In Context

Putting the great unravel into the overall context, *Figure 32 Trading Trail Draw-Down from Previous Year Winnings* shows the Trading Trail 2010 equity curve adjusted to include the residue of the previous year's winnings that were not re-staked this year. It doesn't look so bad, does it?

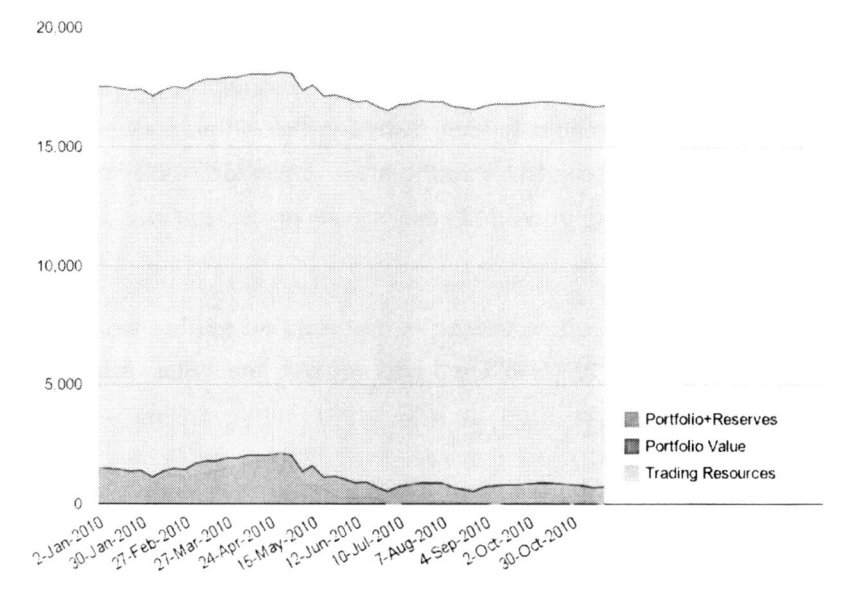

Figure 32 Trading Trail Draw-Down from Previous Year Winnings

Another way to visualise this is via the table shown in *Figure 33 Cumulative Performance to 23 November 2010*, which shows the cumulative performance over two years. In this table you can see that even my 50% drawdown this year reduced the cumulative return to a still-very-spectacular 2775%, all because, having turned £600 into £18,000 in the previous year, I did not assume that in the latest year I would be able to turn the £18,000 into *half a million pounds*. So I didn't bet the farm!

Year	Seed Capital	Portfolio Value	Profit	Profit %	Cumulative Profit	Cumulative Profit %
2009	£ 600.00	£ 18,000.00	£17400	2900.00%	£17400	2900.00%
2010	£ 1,500.00	£ 748.20	-£751.8	-50.12%	£16648.2	2774.70%

Figure 33 Cumulative Performance to 23 November 2010

In fact, even if I had bet the farm (i.e. the full £18,000) in the latest year, and suffered the same 50% draw-down, the cumulative performance would still have been in the order of 1500% over two years.

Lessons from the Great Unravel

As I've already suggested, my eagerness to re-establish my positions in the new account after having cashed-in the old account perfectly was a big contributory factor to the draw-down. Ultimately this was my fault, but I plead 'pressure to perform' as my mitigation.

In the first few weeks of the Trading Trail I undertook some madcap index day trading before settling on my position trading strategy as the theme of the blog. While I did recover the initial losses (by position trading) to show a 60% profit before selling out and switching accounts, I feel that my pre-meltdown profit might have been significantly greater had it not been for the initial index-trading-induced drawdown.

In the context of the phrase "only invest what you can afford to lose", I have often said that if you can afford to lose a lot of money then you probably will. Upon cashing out perfectly at the end of April I was awash with trading funds, so one a sense I did have a lot of money that I could afford to lose... so I did. When I subsequently found myself precipitously low on trading funds, I was much more careful, and as a result the portfolio stabilised and started to recover. I re-learned a lesson that I had learnt before; a lesson that serves to reinforce my belief in a strategy that aims to make *big gains from small stakes* rather than risking a big portfolio in pursuit of a modest gain.

Finally, I suffered one or two 'black swan' events including a trade on Connaught on which I lost a massive (relative to my account size) £70 loss due to slippage. In this case I'm not complaining, but *explaining*. While such events had a negative effect my performance, they demonstrated perfectly how important it is to diversify *across positions* and *over time*.

Trading Trail, the Fight-back

They say that *optimism is hoping for the best* whereas *confidence is being able to handle the worst*. I handled the worst (for my strategy) in 2010 and stayed in the game long enough to stabilize my portfolio and begin that fight-back that you can see in *Figure 34 Trading Trail, the Fight-back*.

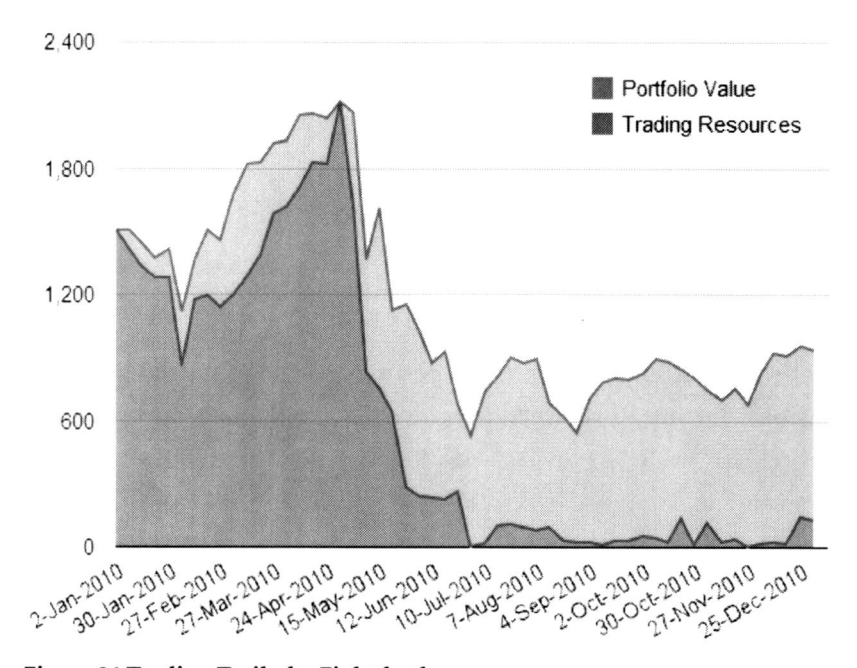

Figure 34 Trading Trail, the Fight-back

The fight-back has seen my portfolio value increase by almost 78% in the six months since the low point in July 2010.

It may be interesting for me to point out that the fight-back coincided with the introduction of my Position Trading Cockpit spreadsheet (see Chapter 11 – Automating the Strategy) that helps keep track of my previously stopped-out positions and the day's biggest fallers.

I took my final snapshot of the equity curve at 31 December 2010. At this time the cumulative performance since the original 2009 documented trading run was as shown in *Figure 35 Cumulative Performance to 31 December 2010*.

Year	Seed Capital	Portfolio Value	Profit	Profit %	Cumulative Profit	Cumulative Profit %
2009	£ 600.00	£ 18,000.00	£17400	2900.00%	£17400	2900.00%
2010	£ 1,500.00	£ 934.79	-£565.21	-37.68%	£16834.79	2805.80%

Figure 35 Cumulative Performance to 31 December 2010

Note that the 38% end-of-year draw down represented a 38% reduction from only the 2010 seed capital and not a 38% reduction of the entire cumulative profit from 2009. Nonetheless, even if I had re-staked the full £18,000 from 2009 as seed capital in 2010 (which I didn't), and if I had drawn down by the same 38%, I would still have been left with more than £11,000 – some 18 times my original £600 seed capital deployed in 2009.

On Luck and Skill

When my strategy produces a positive outcome it would be only natural for me to attribute it to my *skill*, with a negative outcome being the result of *sheer bad luck*. Sceptics would attribute a positive outcome to *sheer good luck*, and would put a negative outcome down to my (lack of) *skill*.

So, what is luck and what is skill?

My personal belief is that most if not all of our profits are 'lucky' in the sense that we cannot accurately predict – and certainly not assure – an outsize return of 3000% in any given year. And the results documented here prove it. All we can do is to make sure that we are on board and that we hold on for the ride... wherever it takes us.

I believe that our losses are a result of skill (or lack of it) because whereas we can't control the size of our gains, we can absolutely control the size of our losses through prudent position sizing, placement of stop orders, and occasionally knowing when to walk away. And the results documented here prove it. If we take care of the downside and let the upside take care of itself then we *might get lucky*.

Future Proof

While I believe this position trading approach to be 'future proof' (i.e. it will work, or at least not fail too badly, in the future) that's not what I intended to convey by this section heading.

My intention was to consider the ways in which I might produce additional proofs in the future.

I could run a similar documented trial in a regular brokerage account rather than a spread betting account. All of the techniques would be applicable, with the possible exception of *leverage*. And while I do already operate one or more regular brokerage accounts, they are currently not documented and publicised.

I could also run future trials using the same techniques on additional financial instruments; by position-trading indices, commodities, and maybe even currencies.

If and when I decide to run such additional public trials, I will communicate these via my *position trading web site* trailed in *Chapter 13 – Visit Me*.

I might also consider more comprehensive back-testing of the approach, as suggested by one of my manuscript reviewers. But I have a couple of problems with this:

- Back-testing lends itself to a fully mechanical system, which this position trading approach *almost is* but not entirely. There are elements of personal judgement regarding position entry (what to buy, and when) and trade maintenance (how closely to trail those stop orders) which cannot easily be encoded in a back-testing script.

- It is far too easy to optimise variables such as trailing stop distances so that the approach appears to work under historic conditions; but which proves nothing in terms of future market conditions. In Chapter 14 of my book *Financial Trading Patterns* I showed how back-testing could *prove* and also *disprove* the same mechanical index-trading system based on trailing stop orders; and I showed how sensitive the results were to the initial parameters (i.e. the choice of stop distance).

- Back tests do not reveal the negative effect of emotions such as *fear* and *greed*, which can have a real effect on the real trading decisions made by real traders in real time.

My preference is to forward-test my trading rules in near-real-time, using *real money* and with the threat of a *real risk of loss*.

While I was fortunate enough to have benefitted from favourable market conditions for long traders during my first public demonstration, *I could not have known this in advance*. Each time I have been willing to put my neck (and money) on the line by committing to a public trial with no prior knowledge of what the markets would throw at me. Even during the unravelling phase of the 2010 Trading Trail.

How many trading authors do that?

Will it Work for You?

Obviously I can't guarantee that you will achieve comparable results by following the techniques described in this book. For one thing: despite my best efforts *in this book*, you might not practice these techniques *exactly as I do*.

POSITION TRADING

I recommend that you don't follow my trading rules exactly as I do, nor follow anyone's trading system slavishly for that matter. I firmly believe that a successful trading system is a very personal thing: developed through years of trial-and-error, formalised by keeping your own trading journal, and adapted to your own personality type.

Come to think of it, *I* might not practice the techniques exactly as described here. And at times, I haven't. Successful trading is an *emotional* as well as *mechanical* process, and I may be at times just as emotional as the next man… or woman. I'm continually fighting my emotions; and always learning the important lessons offered by the ever-changing market conditions.

Those *market conditions* really are changing all the time. As the editor of my *Stop Orders* book pointed out to me at the time of my first demonstration portfolio, the period between March and September 2009 was an exceptional time in the markets. Look at *Figure 36 FTSE 100 March to September 2009* to see what he meant.

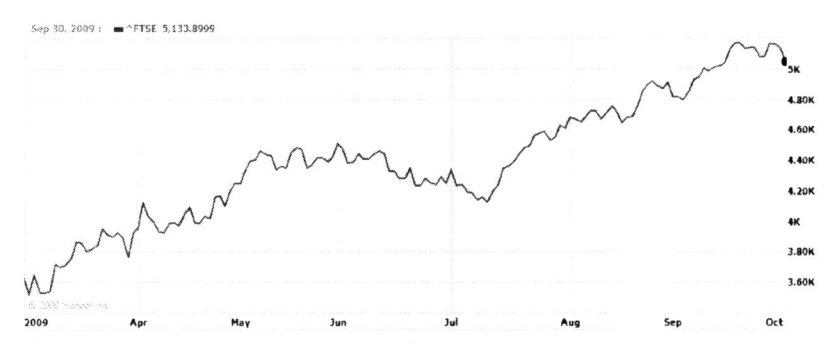

Figure 36 FTSE 100 March to September 2009

Having set your expectations sufficiently low in terms of reproducibility, there are two very good reasons why I think that taking inspiration from my position trading results should be beneficial:

- The approach is designed to magnify the effects of a favourable market thanks to *leverage* and *pyramiding*. Note that the FTSE 100 index increased by about 40% in the period shown whereas my *portfolio value* in the same period increased by some 3000%.

- The approach is designed to limit the negative effects of an unfavourable market thanks to effective *position sizing* (not committing too much too soon) and *stop orders* (to cut losses early). We aim to lose little or no money; and expect to lose no more than our initial trading fund (£300 and £1000 respectively in this chapter's two examples).

So while double-, triple-, or even quadruple-digit returns cannot be assured, nor maybe even expected, we should at least aim to preserve as much capital as possible during adverse market conditions. I repeat: we should take care of the downside, and let the upside take care of itself.

Scaling Up

My public trading accounts have been real accounts, but small ones.

So having made a profit of some £18,000 between two accounts in 2009, and then £550 profit in just over three months in the *Trading Trail* account, at all times utilising very small amounts of initial capital, I might have impressed you a little but not convinced you to give up the day job to trade fulltime.

Unless, of course, you scale up the results and conclude that turning £600 into £18,000 is equivalent to turning £6000 into £180,000; or that turning £1000 into £1550 is akin to turning £10,000 into £15,500.

The problem is that when scaling up the results you also need to scale up the draw-downs along the way. Notice in *Figure 26 Equity Curve for*

3000% in Six Months that between mid-May and mid-July the portfolio value fell from around £7000 to around £4500; which is equivalent to a fall from £70,000 to £45,000 on a bigger account – a massive £30,000 fall.

Also consider that at its lowest point, my 2010 Trading Trail account was drawn down some 65%. So the question is: could you watch 65% of your portfolio slip away and still sleep well at night? I thought not, which is why I was right to re-stake a mere fraction of my 2009 winnings during 2010. Never mind the fact that I *could have* turned my £18,000 winnings into half a million pounds by securing another outsize 3000% return. I could have lost it all, and I nearly did, pro rata.

Don't be greedy!

So What Does This Prove?

Logicians would argue that the results presented here actually prove *nothing*. However many successes we experience in support of a theory, it takes only one failure to disprove it.

As far as I know, this positive proof problem is intractable; we simply can't solve it.

But having tried my hand at many trading approaches before settling on this one, and having proven *to my own satisfaction* that the other approaches don't work, this is what I am left with. And so far – it works!

Are You Ready to Give Up the Day Job?

After having dabbled in the markets for a number of years, perfecting my strategy, and losing a not-insignificant amount of money in the process, while holding down a lucrative career as an IT consultant, a few years ago I gave up the day job so as to trade and write fulltime.

Most of the time it is possible for me to make more money from tax-free trading than from writing; but the latter is useful as a source of potentially taxable 'employment' income that counts towards my future state pension and other employment-funded state benefits – which I hope I don't need, but you never know – and which comes in handy when a mortgage provider or other organization asks about my employment status or requests to see some 'pay-slips'.

Aside from this technicality, I have essentially given up the day job in order to trade full-time.

Are you ready too? If so, I'd like to dissuade you by suggesting that you should not give up the day job to trade full-time:

- Until you really have perfected your system, which could involve losing a lot of money (as I did) before you do perfect it.

- If you cannot cope with the inevitable draw-downs that occur from time to time.

- If you do not have a skill that you can deploy on a freelance basis while trading: to supplement your trading income when trading is bad, to secure your employment-funded state benefits, or simply to get you out of the house once in a while for the sake of your sanity.

If you decide to ignore this final advice, and go for it yourself, then I wish you luck. And I hope this book helps you.

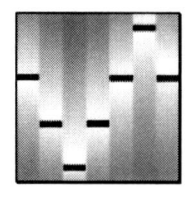

11 – Automating the Strategy

As a former IT consultant and software developer I am always keen to discover ways of automating my trading strategies, but not for the sake of it. Any technical solution I devise must address a genuine need, and where possible should be reproducible by, or accessible to, ordinary mortals – by which I mean 'not computer geeks'. I hope that the solution(s) I present in this chapter on consistent with that ethos.

What to Automate

Two aspects of the Position Trading strategy are crying out for automation: the daily *biggest losers (and gainers) list* and the *'stop-out list '(aka 'sold list')*, both of which were discussed in *Chapter 7 – On Stock Picking*.

Biggest Losers (and gainers)

I'd like to see today's percentage rise or fall of every FTSE All Share stock all in one place, with some kind of traffic light colouring that indicates which stocks are candidates for new long positions and which stocks should be left alone (or sold short). I'd like a solution rather like the spreadsheet shown in *Figure 37 Position Trading Cockpit, Live Prices*.

	A	B	C	D	E	F	G	H	I	J	K
1	3IN.L	3I INFRASTRUCTURE	114	-0.10	249087	-0.09%	http://www.google.co.uk/finance?q=LON:3IN				
2	Symbol	Name	Price	Change	Volume	Change%					
3	3IN.L	3I INFRASTRUCTURE	114	-0.10	249087	-0.09%	http://www.google.co.uk/finance?q=LON:3IN				
4	888.L	888 HOLDINGS	45.75	0.50	189289	1.10%	http://www.google.co.uk/finance?q=LON:888				
5	AAIF.L	ABERDEEN ASIAN INC	164.75	3.25	83240	2.01%	http://www.google.co.uk/finance?q=LON:AAIF				
6	AAL.L	ANGLO AMERICAN	2733.5	92.00	2163003	3.48%	http://www.google.co.uk/finance?q=LON:AAL				
7	AAS.L	ABERDEEN ASIAN SMLR	642	-5.00	14089	-0.77%	http://www.google.co.uk/finance?q=LON:AAS				
8	ABD.L	ABERDEEN NEW DAWN	908	2.50	23620	0.28%	http://www.google.co.uk/finance?q=LON:ABD				
9	ABF.L	ASSOCIAT BRIT FOODS	1059	11.00	341515	1.05%	http://www.google.co.uk/finance?q=LON:ABF				
10	ABG.L	AFRICAN BARR GOLD	631	15.00	398162	2.44%	http://www.google.co.uk/finance?q=LON:ABG				
11	ABR.L	ABSOLUT RET TST-PRP	113	0.00	13808	0.00%	http://www.google.co.uk/finance?q=LON:ABR				
12	ADM.L	ADMIRAL GROUP	1600	-64.00	254908	-3.85%	http://www.google.co.uk/finance?q=LON:ADM				

Figure 37 Position Trading Cockpit, Live Prices

Stop-Out List

I'd like an easy way to maintain a list of recently-closed positions with their last stop-out prices. Each entry should show the latest market price, the percentage rise or fall since stopping out, and a colour-coded indication of which stocks have fallen (for potential long re-entries) of risen (for potential short re-entries) since last stopping out. I'd like a solution rather like the spreadsheet shown in *Figure 38 Position Trading Cockpit, Stop-Out List*.

	A	B	C	D	E	F	G	H
1	HOME.L	HOME RETAIL GROUP	215.6	205	Long	10.6	5.17%	3.70%
2		Name	Price	Last Stop Out	Want to...	Change Since	Change% Since Stop	%Change Today
3	HOME.L	HOME RETAIL GROUP	215.6	205	Long	10.6	5.17%	3.70%
4	INCH.L	INCHCAPE	335.1	299	Long	36.1	12.07%	5.76%
5	IPF.L	INTL PERSONAL FIN	282.3	238	Long	44.3	18.61%	5.14%
6	ITV.L	ITV	63.75	49	Long	14.75	30.10%	7.59%
7	LAD.L	LADBROKES	137.4	131	Long	6.4	4.89%	1.85%
8	LOOK.L	LOOKERS	59.9	99999	Long	-99939.1	-99.94%	-0.99%

Figure 38 Position Trading Cockpit, Stop-Out List

Automation Options

At the time of writing, the Yahoo! Finance web site is my preferred free source of the latest stock price data, which is available in a comma-separated-value (CSV) download format that lends itself to automatic processing.

In terms of automatic processing we have a few options. Having written a couple of books on the subject, I'm quite interested in the power of Yahoo! Pipes as a technology for reading, manipulating, and re-presenting web data.

POSITION TRADING

In *Figure 39 Yahoo! Pipes, Latest Prices* you can see a snippet of the output from a Yahoo! Pipe that I put together quickly to show the latest price, today's price change, percentage price change, and volume traded for every FTSE All-Share stock.

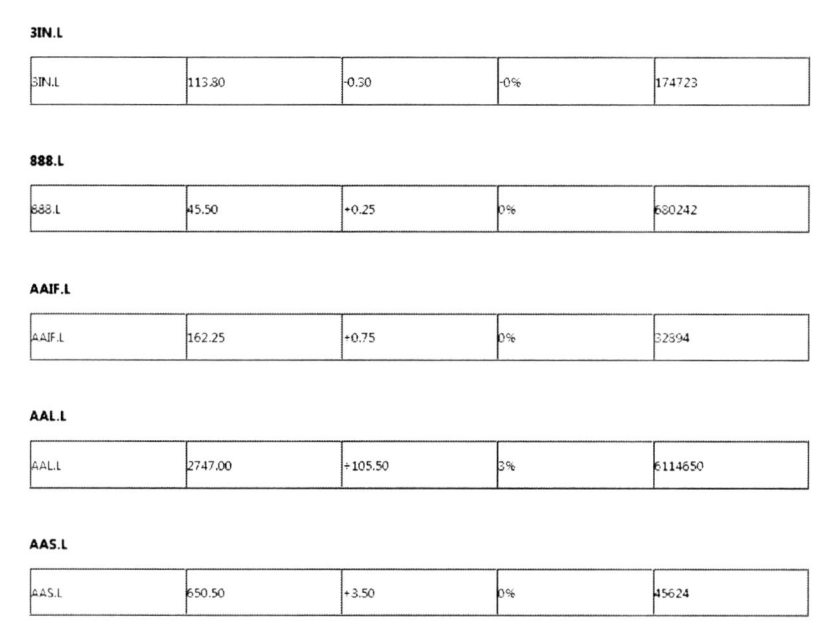

3IN.L

| 3IN.L | 113.80 | -0.30 | -0% | 174723 |

888.L

| 888.L | 45.50 | +0.25 | 0% | 680242 |

AAIF.L

| AAIF.L | 162.25 | +0.75 | 0% | 32394 |

AAL.L

| AAL.L | 2747.00 | +105.50 | 3% | 6114650 |

AAS.L

| AAS.L | 650.50 | +3.50 | 0% | 45624 |

Figure 39 Yahoo! Pipes, Latest Prices

In *Figure 40 Yahoo! Pipes, Stop-Out Price Changes* you can see a snippet of the output from a Yahoo! Pipe that I put together quickly to show the amount by which each of my recently stopped out stocks has risen or fallen since last stopping out. You can't see it easily in the figure, but when invoking the Pipe I specified the last stop-out prices for two of my previous stock holdings (and it could have been more) by appending this information to the web address as shown in bold here:

```
http://pipes.yahoo.com/pipes/pipe.run?_id=afea53f324d61c8263b4ad
a480856f91&soldlist=BP.L@500,EMG.L@200
```

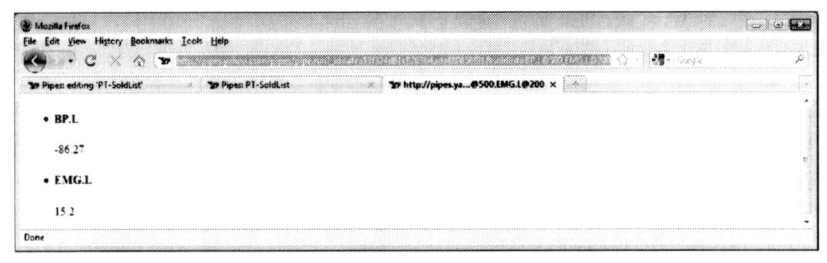

Figure 40 Yahoo! Pipes, Stop-Out Price Changes

While these Yahoo! Pipes solutions do the job and could be made to look nicer, they do not really pass the test of being reproducible by mere mortals. While I think it offers a nice drag-and-drop development environment, you might be left totally bewildered by the construction of a Yahoo! Pipes as shown in *Figure 41 Yahoo! Pipe Example Construction*.

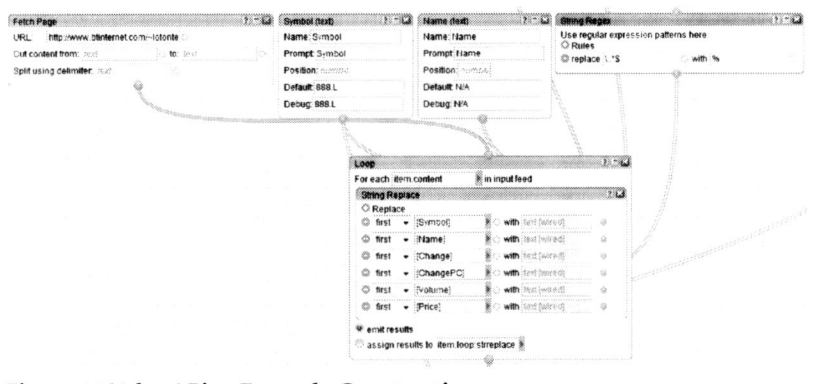

Figure 41 Yahoo! Pipe Example Construction

As an alternative, you may already be familiar with constructing spreadsheets using Microsoft Excel, and you will no doubt prefer the spreadsheet presentation as shown in *Figure 37 Position Trading Cockpit, Live Prices* and *Figure 38 Position Trading Cockpit, Stop-Out List*. So Microsoft Excel is my preferred automation option.

As you will see shortly, there are two key features of Excel that make it ideal for this task: *web queries* (to fetch the live data from Yahoo!

POSITION TRADING

Finance) and *conditional formatting* (to colour-code the potential longs and shorts).

Constructing the Microsoft Excel Spreadsheet

I constructed the example 'Position Trading Cockpit' spreadsheet using Excel 2007 and tested it using Excel 2010, and (from memory) I see no reason why the same solution could not be reproduced using Excel 2003.

The Excel workbook comprises two spreadsheets: the *Live Prices* sheet and the *Stop-Out List* sheet.

The *Live Prices* Sheet

This sheet takes from the Yahoo! Finance web site the live prices (delayed by 15 minutes) for the FTSE All Share stocks.

Source Data

If you navigate to the Yahoo! Finance FTSE All-SHARE web page and click the *Components* link you arrive at the web page that has the URL (web address) of http://uk.finance.yahoo.com/q/cp?s=^FTAS. On this web page you can see for each FTSE All Share stock its stock symbol, name, last trade price, today's change and traded volume.

By clicking the link on this web page labelled *Download to Spreadsheet* you can import the data into Excel by opening the comma-separated-values (CSV) file located at:

```
http://uk.old.finance.yahoo.com/d/quotes.csv?s=@%5EFTAS&f=sl1d1t1c1ohgv&e=.csv
```

The raw data looks like this:

```
3IN.L,114.00, 1:40PM,10/07/2010,-0.10,114.30,114.30,113.80,249087
888.L,45.75, 1:09PM,10/07/2010,+0.50,46.25,46.25,45.50,189289
AAIF.L,164.75,12:46PM,10/07/2010,+3.25,162.00,164.75,162.00,83240
```

```
AAL.L,2747.50, 1:56PM,10/07/2010,+106.00,2751.50,2761.00,2712.50,2063330
AAS.L,642.00, 1:48PM,10/07/2010,-5.00,652.00,659.00,642.00,14089
ABD.L,908.90, 1:26PM,10/07/2010,+3.40,902.00,902.00,902.00,22720
```

All of the required data is in there, including some data – open, high, low and close prices – that are not displayed on the corresponding web page. Conspicuous by its absence is the stock name, which would be very handy for those of us not entirely fluent in stock symbols.

I discovered by trial and error that by manipulating the URL to be as shown below, we can access an alternative raw data file.

```
http://uk.old.finance.yahoo.com/d/quotes.csv?s=@%5EFTAS&e=.csv
```

The alternative presentation usefully includes stock names thus:

```
3IN.L,3I INFRASTRUCTURE,114.00,-0.10,249087
888.L,888 HOLDINGS,45.75,+0.50,189289
AAIF.L,ABERDEEN ASIAN INC,164.75,+3.25,83240
AAL.L,ANGLO AMERICAN,2742.50,+101.00,2113502
AAS.L,ABERDEEN ASIAN SMLR,642.00,-5.00,14089
ABD.L,ABERDEEN NEW DAWN,908.00,+2.50,23620
```

Web Query

We won't import the data into Excel by simply opening the CSV file as just described, because that would be a one-hit snapshot solution. Instead we'll access the data via a web query that refreshes automatically whenever the Excel workbook is opened and at intervals thereafter.

On the Microsoft Excel 2007 menu bar we can click the *Data* tab, and from the *Get External Data* section we can choose the option labelled *From Text*. In the *Import Text File* dialog that appears we can enter the source URL determined earlier.

The three-step *Text Import Wizard* allows us to specify that the data is *Delimited* and to specify the delimiter as a *Comma* as shown in *Figure 42 Text Import Wizard, Step 2*.

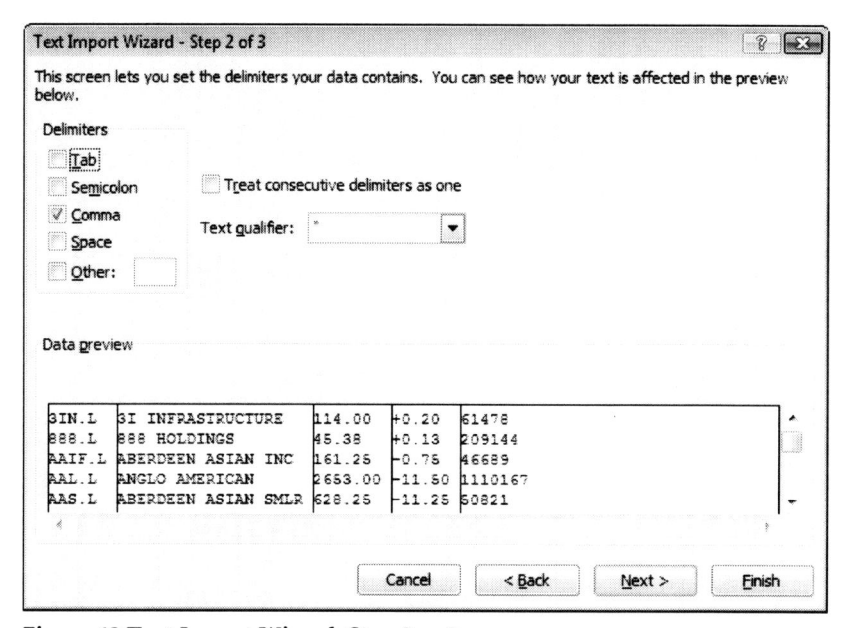

Figure 42 Text Import Wizard, Step 2 or 3

When prompted to choose where to *Import Data* we can access the *External Data Range Properties* dialog so as to specify how frequently the data should be refreshed. See *Figure 43 Import Data, and External Data Range Properties*.

In this case I opt for the data to refresh every time the Excel workbook is opened and then a 5 minute intervals while the workbook remains open.

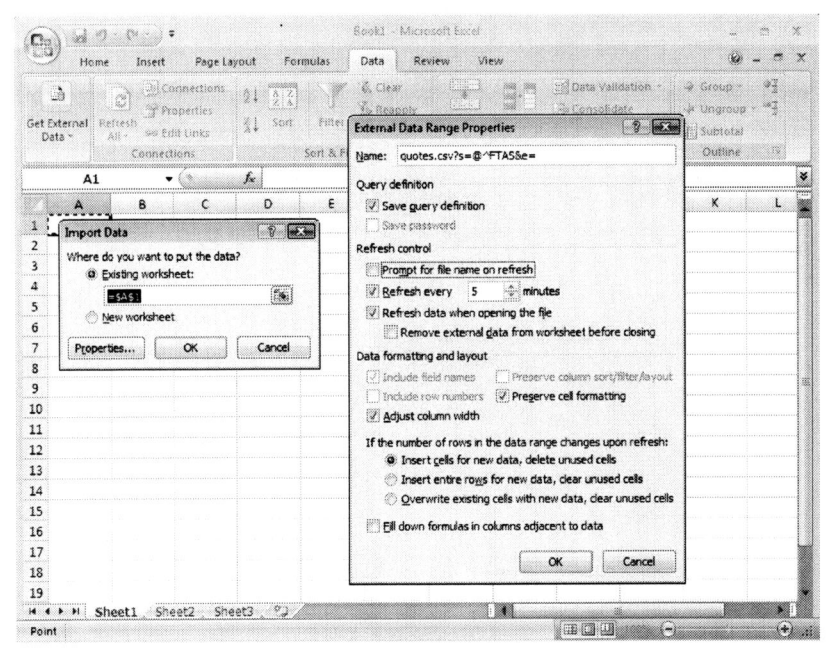

Figure 43 Import Data, and External Data Range Properties

Calculations

In *Figure 44 Calculate % Price Change* you can see the data imported from the previous step and you can see that I have entered a formula into cell F1 to calculate the percentage price change using the values in cells C1 and D1. We would need to copy the same formula into the cells below and we'd need to change the format of column F to display values as *Percentage*.

	SUBSTITUTE		× ✓ fx	=C1/(C1-D1)-1				
	A	B		C	D	E	F	G
1	3IN.L	3I INFRASTRUCTURE		113.8	0	3564	=C1/(C1-D1)-1	
2	888.L	888 HOLDINGS		45.38	0.13	209144		
3	AAIF.L	ABERDEEN ASIAN INC		161.25	-0.75	51679		
4	AAL.L	ANGLO AMERICAN		2652	-12.5	1126294		
5	AAS.L	ABERDEEN ASIAN SMLR		628.25	-11.25	52321		
6	ABD.L	ABERDEEN NEW DAWN		890	-16.5	24988		
7	ABF.L	ASSOCIAT BRIT FOODS		1043	-12	235480		

Figure 44 Calculate % Price Change

Conditional Formatting

As you saw previously in *Figure 37 Position Trading Cockpit, Live Prices* I'd like cells in the *% Change* column to be coloured on a scale from bright red (fallen a lot) through white (hardly changed) to bright blue (risen a lot). I can do this by selecting the entire column and choosing *New Rule* from the *Conditional Formatting* menu as shown in *Figure 45 Conditional Formatting Menu*.

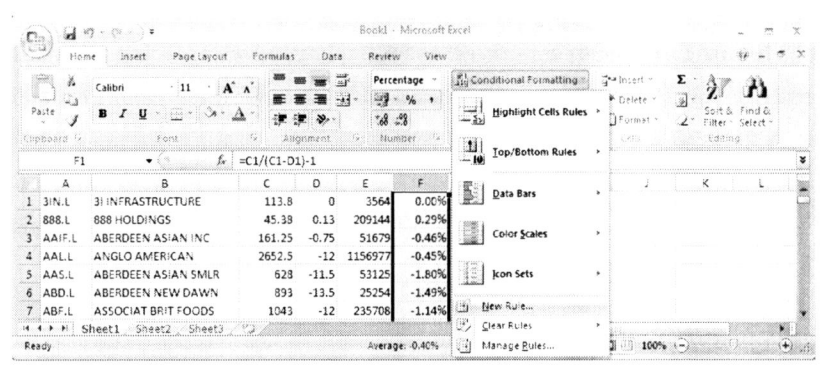

Figure 45 Conditional Formatting Menu

I fill out the *New Formatting Rule* dialog as shown in *Figure 46 Conditional Formatting Rule*, so that the brightest red applies to stocks that have fallen by 10% today and that the brightest blue applies to stocks that have gone up by 10%.

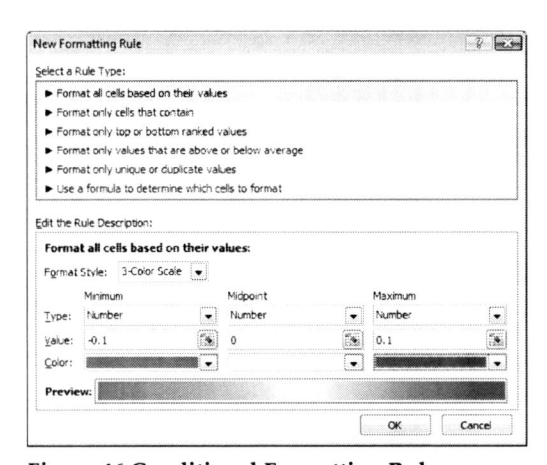

Figure 46 Conditional Formatting Rule

You already know what the end result looks like.

Adapting the Data Source for Other Markets

As described here, the Live Prices tab displays latest prices and price changes for the FTSE All-Share stocks obtained from this source URL:

`http://uk.old.finance.yahoo.com/d/quotes.csv?s=@%5E`**`FTAS`**`&e=.csv`

In theory it is possible to adapt the solution for S&P 500 stocks, DAX stocks, or those from any other market simply by replacing the code **FTAS** in the URL with another code such as **GSPC** (S&P 500) or **GDAXI** (DAX). In some cases this will not work, for example because USA companies tend to have the text ", inc" appended to their names – which has a tendency to mess up the comma-separated source data because of the extra comma.

This problem could be solved by reverting to the original source data URL that does not include stock names in the output data. The original source data URL was:

`http://uk.old.finance.yahoo.com/d/quotes.csv?s=@%5EFTAS&f=sl1d1t1c1ohgv&e=.csv`

The *Stop-Out List* Sheet

This sheet allows you to record the price at which you last stopped-out of a stock, and whether you're looking for an opportunity to go long (at a lower price than your last stop-out) or short (at a higher price than your last stop-out).

Stock Symbol Pull-Down List and Stock Name

In the first column of this sheet I'd like to be provided with a pull-down list of the stock symbols of the FTSE All Share index; i.e. a choice of all the stock symbols available in the *Live Prices* sheet. This can be achieved by selecting the cell or column and choosing *Data Validation* from the *Data* menu. The dialog shown in *Figure 47 Data*

Validation for Pull-Down List allows you to specify a *List* with an *In-cell dropdown* as the *Validation criteria,* and to specify the first column of the Live Prices sheet as the *Source* of the stock symbols. The source is specified as:

`=LivePrices!$A:$A`

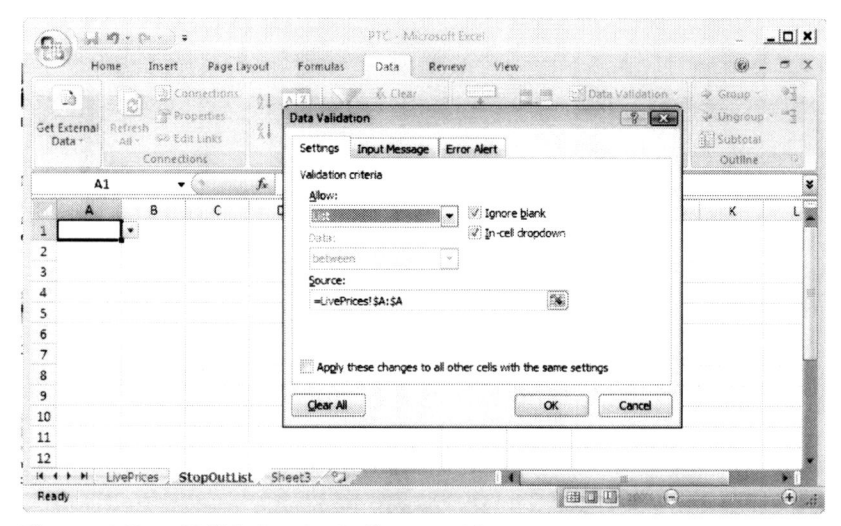

Figure 47 Data Validation for Pull-Down List

With the selections allowed in cell A1 of this sheet limited to the stock symbols in the first column of the Live Prices spreadsheet, we can now enter the following formula into cell B1 of *this sheet* so as to retrieve the corresponding company name from column B of the Live Prices sheet.

`=INDEX(LivePrices!$B:$B,MATCH(A1,LivePrices!$A:$A,0))`

Long and Short Selection

In column D I'd like the user to enter (or select from a pull-down list) the text "Long" or "Short" and for this text to be coloured red if "Long" or blue if "Short". *Figure 48 Long and Short Formatting Rule* provides an example formatting rule to colour the cell red if the text is "Long".

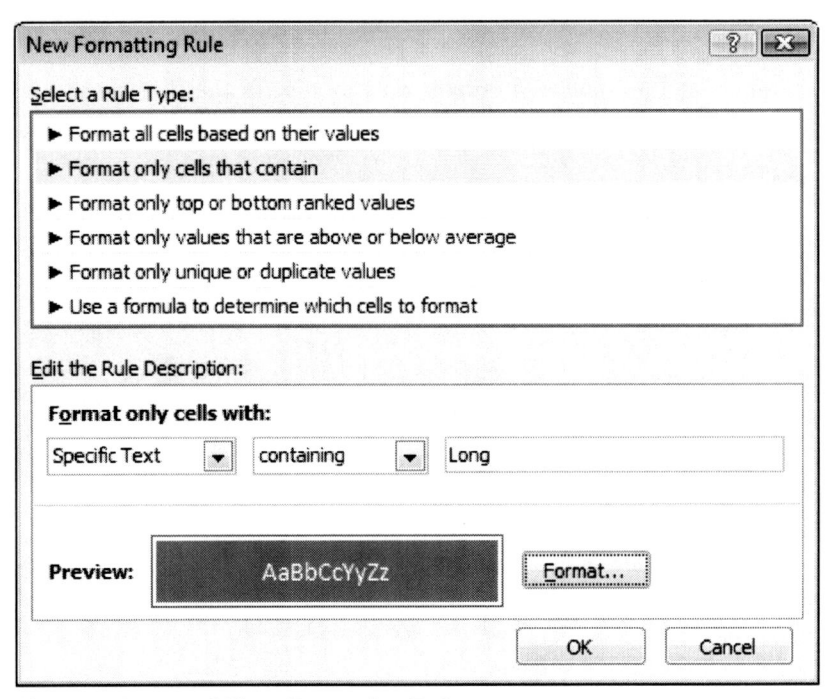

Figure 48 Long and Short Formatting Rule

This column will remind us that we're looking for fallen (red) stocks for a possible long re-entry and risen (blue) stocks for a possible short re-entry.

Figure 49 Stop-Out List, Partially Complete shows the story so far. Whenever one of our positions stops out we can select its stock symbol in column A, the stock name will be retrieved automatically into column B, and our choice of Long or Short text in column D will be coloured red or blue as appropriate.

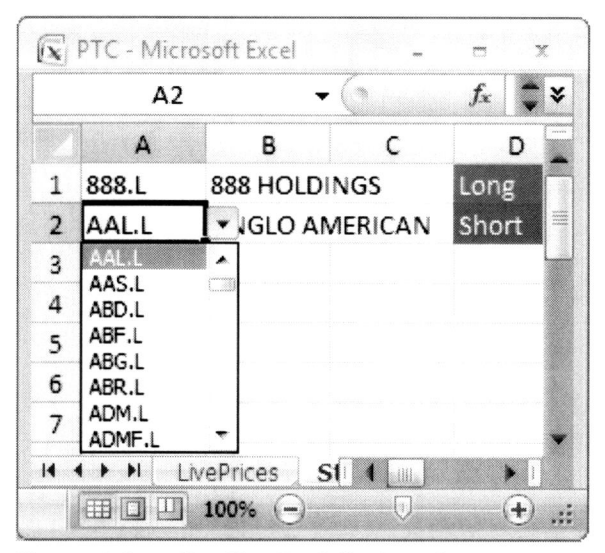

Figure 49 Stop-Out List, Partially Complete

Last Stop-Out, Live Price, and %Change Since Stop-Out

If you're wondering why I skipped column C, it's because that's where I'd like to enter my last stop-out price for each stock. There's no fancy formula because it's simply an empty cell for the user to enter a value.

In column E we'll retrieve the current (delayed 15 mins) live price for the stock from the Live Prices sheet, using this formula:

`=INDEX(LivePrices!$C:$C,MATCH(A1,LivePrices!$A:$A,0))`

In column F we calculate the percentage change from the last stop-out price using this formula:

`=(E1-C1)/C1`

We apply conditional formatting to column F so that % price discounts are shown red and % price mark-ups are shown blue, on a sliding scale, as we did for column F of the *Live Prices* sheet.

Stop-Out List, Complete

Adding a header row completes the Stop-Out List spreadsheet as shown in *Figure 50 Stop-Out List, Complete*.

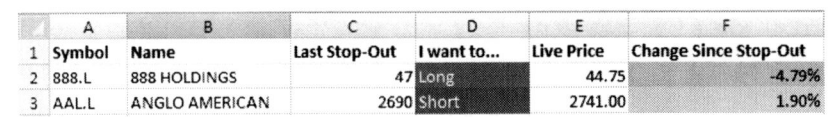

	A	B	C	D	E	F
1	Symbol	Name	Last Stop-Out	I want to...	Live Price	Change Since Stop-Out
2	888.L	888 HOLDINGS	47	Long	44.75	-4.79%
3	AAL.L	ANGLO AMERICAN	2690	Short	2741.00	1.90%

Figure 50 Stop-Out List, Complete

All Done For You

By following the instructions in this chapter you should be able to construct your own Microsoft Excel workbook to search for *new position candidates* and to automate you *Stop-Out List*. If you don't want to put in the work to implement these steps yourself you will be pleased to hear that I have done it for you.

You can gain access to the *Position Trading Cockpit* workbook from:

`www.lotontech.com/positiontradingcockpit`

Using this spreadsheet has saved me a great deal of time... and money!

Not Only Microsoft Excel

Microsoft Excel may be the best tool for the job, but what if you don't have it?

Although the solution is not quite so elegant, it is perfectly possible to replicate the idea using the free-to-use on-line Google Docs spreadsheet application that is accessible at docs.google.com.

You can see the Google Docs version of the Position Trading Cockpit in *Figure 51 Google Docs Position Trading Cockpit, Live Prices* and *Figure 52 Google Docs Position Trading Cockpit, Stop-Out List*.

POSITION TRADING

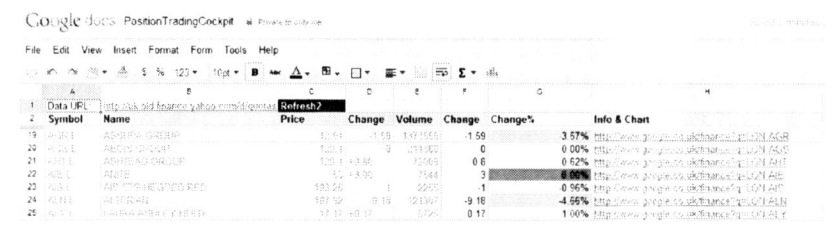

Figure 51 Google Docs Position Trading Cockpit, Live Prices

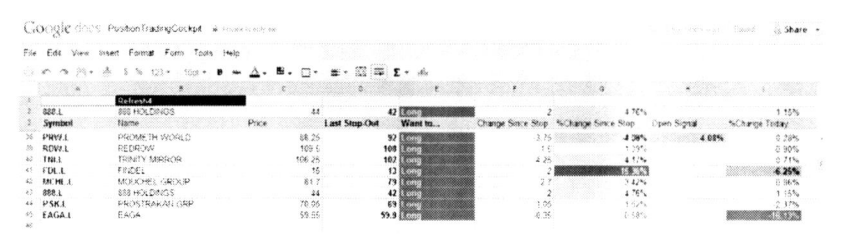

Figure 52 Google Docs Position Trading Cockpit, Stop-Out List

I can access the Google Docs version of the Position Trading Cockpit from any computer anywhere using nothing more sophisticated than my web browser.

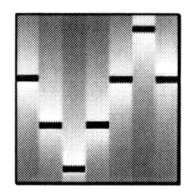

12 – Q & A

In the course of running the daily Trading Trail blog throughout 2010 I received a steady stream of comments from my blog followers. Here I present some of those questions along with my responses. In some cases the responses are verbatim, exactly how I posted them originally, but in some cases they have been edited, re-worded or even re-thought for the sake of clarity.

Comment about initial risks limited to 1%

'A' asked me at the outset whether I would be limiting my risk on each position to a fixed percentage of trading funds, for example a 1% initial risk on each trade.

Response

Not religiously so, but when placing £1-per-point bets in an account funded with only £1000 I would tend to limit my initial risk to £10 per bet.

Comment about variable initial risks

'G' pointed out that a £10 risk on a 10p stock represents a 100% risk on a £1-per-point spread bet whereas on a 100p stock it represents only a 10% risk. Also, that if the 10p stock doubles in price I make only £10 profit compared with £100 profit if the 100p stock doubles in price.

Response

On the first point: it's a £10 risk in both cases and the percentage doesn't matter. On the second point: to equalise the upside potential on all trades would require some additional calculations, periodic 'rebalancing', and might necessitate placing fractional trades on some instruments (e.g. £0.25-per-point) which some platforms do not allow. Also, there should be numerous opportunities to pyramid into a 10p stock on its journey to becoming a 100p stock so it may well attract a higher stake en route.

Comment about risk calculations

'G' commented that my stating of risks as merely 'how much I stand to lose if my stop is hit' is only half the equation. As any good IT project manager knows: **risk = probability × impact**.

Response

My definition of risk coincided with the definition used on the spread betting platform that I was operating at the time, so it made for clearer blog posts if I didn't deviate from that definition. Although we try to assess the *probability* of a stop-out or a profit when placing a trade, we can't really ever know the *probability* except in retrospect, so there is an argument for assuming a 50/50 probability (either it will stop out or it won't) on every trade. This takes probability out of the equation, and leaves the *impact* which we can define very precisely.

Comment about technical vs. fundamental analysis

A reader asked: "Please can you explain the thinking behind each trade, i.e. what factors made you buy or sell? Are you using technical or fundamental analysis?"

Response

While fundamental analysis may be beneficial when practised properly, the simple screening of stocks on analysts' forecasts of fundamental measures like Dividend Yield, P/E, and PEG is in my opinion very dubious.

I make my decisions mainly based on price action, which I guess falls under the heading of technical analysis, but without all the complications of RSI, ADX etc. etc. Simply put: if the price of a stock has fallen significantly today, it *might* bounce back up in the short term; if it is down something like 80% from its historic high price then it is *probably* good value in the long term.

I use words like *might* and *probably* because nothing is certain, which is why I think that money- and risk- management is more important than clever stock picking.

Comments about becoming profitable

Many readers asked me about how to become a profitable trader.

Response

The first problem is how we define 'profitable'. Notch up a small profit every day, like a day trader? Make £18,000 in the first year and lose £1000 in the second year so as to be profitable over the two-year cycle? The best definition of 'profitable' that I ever read was simply "Could you take more out of your trading account today than the total amount you ever put in?"

As for the question itself, my answer is:

> I have read many, many, trading and investment books over the years. They have given me lots of inspiration and ideas that have been incorporated into my approach. But not one of

them has made me profitable in itself, any more than anyone ever learns to ride a bicycle by reading about it in a book. You learn to ride a bike by falling off a few times and hoping that you discover a sense of balance before killing yourself. The most important thing is to *stay in the game* long enough for good things to start happening.

Comment about buying fallers

A reader asked "Could you comment on why you look for trades in the losers' lists and not shares that are doing well?"

Response

By the time you see that a stock is doing well, it may be too late, and it may well fall (very demoralising) as soon as you buy it. I'm looking at least for an initial bounce on a stock that may have over-reacted downwards... and looking hopefully for much more down the line if the stock is trading at a mere fraction of its former glory. My initial tight stop and small position size ensures that I escape relatively unscathed if I am wrong.

Comment about re-buying lower

A reader commented that if I re-purchase a stock that has previously stopped-out, even at a lower price, I am effectively lowering my stop level – which is a big trading 'no-no'.

Response

Suppose a stock falls from 100p to 90p and stops me out for a loss of £10. If it falls further and I can re-purchase at 80p then I have skipped an additional £10 loss (compared with simply holding) and notionally made £10 additional profit if the stock recovers. If the price rises soon after my 'stop out' then I will 'miss out' but at least my loss will have been capped at the initial £10. But I acknowledge the risk of buying lower and lower and suffering a 'death by a thousand cuts'.

Comments about guaranteed stops and slippage

Several readers asked about whether guaranteed stops were worth the additional spread and / or fee in terms of the extra protection.

Response

I demonstrated in the Trading Trail how sometimes a guaranteed stop could yield a 'whipsaw profit' whereby the trading platform has to stop you out of a gapped-down stock at a higher price than the price at which you can now re-purchase. However, guaranteed stops can be problematic in terms of increased spread, minimum stop distances, inability to adjust out-of-hours, and unavailability on some instruments.

I tend to take an actuarial approach to using non-guaranteed stops on a large number of small positions so that no single slippage can wipe me out.

Comment about trading the news

A reader posted a very specific question about his position in Cable & Wireless on which he had managed to trail his stop order to break-even. In the light of negative news, should he cash-in or let it ride?

Response

I would not presume to advise on a specific trade, but in general I would let the stop order do its job and don't attempt to pre-empt it by 'trading the news'.

Comment about determining stop levels

A reader asked me whether I determine stop levels according to volatility (as implied in my Stop Orders book) or according to support, and whether I trail stop orders according to volatility until they have reached break-even.

Response

My 'Stop Orders' book described stop orders more generally in the contexts of different trading styles, whereas the Trading Trail (and this book) focuses on stop orders in the context of my Position Trading strategy.

My initial stop levels are determined mainly by support, and I try to trail my stop orders cautiously or not at all until they reach break-even. Thereafter, I attempt to trail my stop orders no closer than 15% below the prevailing market price but also respectful of support prices.

Comment about trading indices

The same questioner asked me about why I was trading individual equities rather than indices.

Response

In a small £1000 account it is difficult to trade four-digit indices with minimal risk unless overly-tight stop orders are used. The Position Trading strategy also depends on using diversification – not the kind provided by indices – across a large number of positions. In a small account this must necessarily be a large number of low-priced positions.

Comment about trading breakouts

'John' asked me whether I would short a stock that had fallen through support, or buy a stock that has broken upwards through resistance.

Response

I would more likely buy a stock that had bounced upwards from support and short a stock that had bounced downwards from resistance so as to benefit from at least the 'swing'. I would likely continue holding through resistance (on a long trade) or through support (on a short trade) in order to benefit from a potential longer term trend.

Comment about volatile markets and risk capital

At one point a reader asked me: "If your aim is not to lose money, why risk 25% of your capital when markets are so jumpy?"

Response

At the time of this question my 25% risk capital was spread across roughly 25 positions thus giving an average risk of 1% per position. My total risk capital this year was also a mere fraction of my banked profit from the previous year.

As for markets being jumpy: that's when some people make a lot of money!

Comment about share consolidations

Someone asked me a question about whether it is possible to bank a significant quick profit in a spread betting account when a share prices rises massively on a share consolidation.

Response

Sadly, no, just as you would not expect to be disadvantaged by a share split. When a share consolidates or splits the spread betting company will adjust your stake in the same proportion if they can, or they will close your position at the old price. You must check your stop levels after such an event, as these may or may not have been adjusted by the broker.

Comment about pyramiding

A reader commented that an accrued profit in an existing position is not sufficient to justify pyramiding into that position.

Response

I agree that it is not *sufficient*, but it is *necessary*. Don't pyramid a position simply because a good profit is locked in. On the other hand, don't pyramid a position *unless a good profit is locked in*. In other words, try to risk only accrued profits or (to put it another way) *other people's money*.

Comment about concentration vs. diversification

At one point a commentator asked me: what was the point of holding 40 fallen knives with tight stops when I could concentrate on 20 fallen knives with wider stops for the same total risk?

Response

I didn't plan to hold 40, 20, or any other number of fallen knives; I just caught them when I spotted them. The subtlety in the original question was that I could perhaps 'cherry pick' the twenty best prospects, but I argue that we can't possibly know which are the best prospects except in hindsight. My approach to pyramiding should help me 'pick the winners' by increasing my stakes in positions that perform well.

Comment about win / loss ratio

'L' commented that although in my strategy I would get a much bigger winner, the pain of sustaining the numerous small cuts is hard for most to endure. He said that his psychology would require a 50% success rate so that he did not give up at exactly the markets turned around.

Response

It's perfectly true that if you win $100 on at least 51% of your trades and lose $100 on no more than 49% of your trades then you'll come out ahead over time. But what if you win $50 on 51% of your trades and lose $100 on 49% of your trades? My approach to cutting losses and running profits means that I don't need to have a more-than-50% win rate, but it's not foolproof and it can lead to a death by a thousand cuts unless one has sufficient capital to withstand one-thousand-and-one cuts.

Comment about account size

When my Trading Trail was at its lowest point 'L' suggested that if I managed my money so poorly in a small account, how could I be confident about managing a large account?

Response

Although it's not ideal, I don't see a big problem with losing 50% of the trading funds in a small £1000 account – i.e. losing £500 – if the remaining £500 could turn into several thousand pounds. Suppose I had a available funds of £18,000 (i.e. a bigger *potential account*) and I lost just £500 by staking only £1000 of the available funds in search of an outsize profit. The 3% draw-down wouldn't be so bad, would it? That's pretty much what I did.

Comment about trend following

'L' suggested that catching falling knives is futile, and totally unnecessary because a simple trend-following system would be more effective and less volatile.

Response

I am a trend follower in the sense that I will hold positions for as long as possible, and possibly pyramid into them while they are trending. I don't establish an initial position *after identifying a trend* because in my experience it's too late. And trends have a nasty habit of petering out as soon as you jump on board. My approach is to buy on weakness and hold (not sell prematurely) on strength.

Comment about stock picking

Blog reader 'Off the lip' complimented me several times on my ability to spot stocks that rose in price almost as soon as I had established my positions.

Response

Yes, I buy stocks in the hope of at least an immediate bounce. But we need to be careful about survivorship and hindsight biases (remembering only the winners and not the losers) and I note that even a >50% 'win rate' is no good if you win £100 on every winner and lose £200 on every loser. Being 'right' is also useless unless you are ready, willing and able to do something about it.

Comment about rising (and falling) tides

One reader pointed out at one point that my equity curve was very similar to that of the FTSE index, so I could have simply bought a FTSE tracker and gone out to play (my words, not his).

Response

While I agree that a "rising tide lifts all boats" (and vice versa) it doesn't mean that a rising boat requires a rising tide. If you believe their historic price charts, the stocks I hold have massively more upside potential than the market as a whole. Any of my positions could significantly outpace the market on some catalyst event such as a takeover bid; and because I would pyramid into a sustained rising tide, the relationship between the FTSE and my portfolio should turn out to be asymmetric.

Comment about overnight financing / rolling charges

A questioner asked me how much of my loss (at that time) could be attributed to overnight financing / rolling charges.

Response

At the time my portfolio value was down by about £700 and the total of the financing charges that I had paid in the previous 3 months was a mere £17.98. This illustrates that in a low interest rate environment the cost of holding rolling spread bets is minimal compared with the losses that could accumulate due to bad trades.

Comment about stop distances

Alan commented: from what little I've read (as a novice) it seems that stops should be kept as tight as possible. Is there a simple way of calculating how far away to place a stop?

Response

In my "Position Trading" approach I set tight stops initially, but I then let them widen as the price rises; before starting to trail them upwards to lock-in accrued profits. Trailing stops too tightly can cause you to stop out too frequently and unnecessarily. Personally I want to stop out quickly, or (ideally) never.

Comment about pyramiding

I don't really follow your logic as regards pyramiding. The market is oblivious to whether or not you already have an unrealised profit in a particular share so I can't see why you should take into account the fact that you have such a profit when making a decision to take a new position.

Response

It's more to do with 'money management', and the fact that if I have enough profit locked-in to an existing position thanks to my trailed stop order – enough profit to cover my risk on an additional position, that is – then the additional position is in a sense 'risk free', or is risking "other people's money". It may well be true that another stock is more attractive, in which case I would use the profit locked-in on Stock A to create a new (or additional) risk-free position in Stock B.

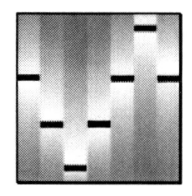

13 – Visit Me

If you want to find out more about position trading, and interact with me and other position trading practitioners, then please do visit my dedicated web site accessible at:

`www.lotontech.com/positiontrading` or

`http://onpositiontrading.blogspot.com`

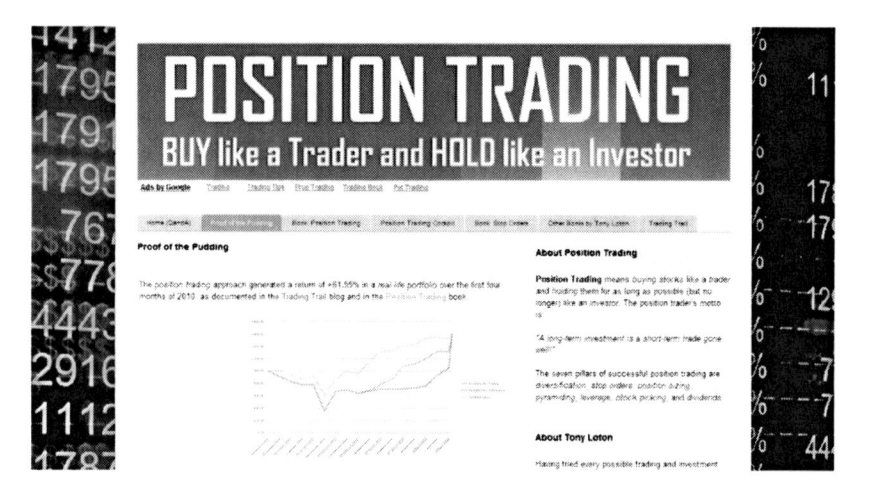

I look forward to seeing you.

While you're online, why not post a review of *this book* on Amazon for the benefit of other potential readers? But please, be kind!

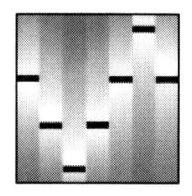

Appendix A – Support and Resistance

My position trading strategy employs very few technical indicators, and even fewer (if any) fundamental ratios. The strategy is based on a simple assessment of price action, combined with good money management throughout the life of each trade.

The one technical indicator I do use a lot is the notion of price *support*. And with the inclusion of price *resistance*, I suppose it can be counted as two indicators.

These indicators influence not only the time and price at which I will establish a new position, but also the initial and trailing stop distance I will maintain at the outset and throughout the life of a trade.

Support

A support level is the price level at which a falling price is more likely to rebound upwards than continue falling. It is the level at which a falling price finds support in the market; and it is deemed to be more credible if the price rebounds upwards from this level more than once.

In *Figure 53 Price Support* you can see that Bloomsbury, the publisher of Harry Potter books, found long-term price support at about 110p between October 2007 and January 2010.

Note that support levels may be found on charts of various timescales; from intra-day to multi-year.

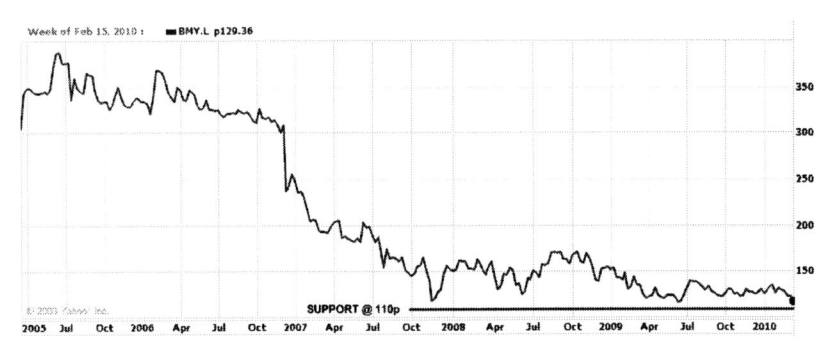

Figure 53 Price Support

When establishing a new long position, I would do so ideally at a price just above a support level, with my initial protective stop order just below the support level.

When trailing my stop orders, usually no closer than 15% below the prevailing market price, I would also be mindful to keep those stop orders below any key support levels.

Resistance

A resistance level is a price level at which a rising price is more likely to rebound downwards than continue rising. It is the level at which a rising price meets resistance in the market; and it is deemed to be more credible if the price rebounds downwards from this level more than once.

In *Figure 54 Price Resistance* you can see that the FTSE 100 index met medium-term price resistance at about 4500 during May and into June 2009.

Note that resistance levels may be found on charts of various timescales; from intra-day to multi-year.

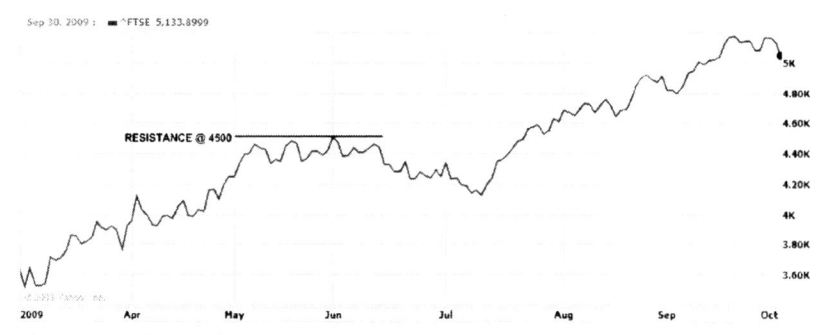

Figure 54 Price Resistance

When establishing a new long position, I would be unlikely to do so at a price near to a resistance level; but I would consider a price just below a resistance level to be a good price at which to *go short*.

When using the partial close-out technique (see *Chapter 7 – On Stock Picking*) I would be inclined to close part of a position at a resistance level.

One Man's Support is Another Man's Resistance

What the long trader regards as a support level, the short trader would regard as a resistance level; and vice-versa.

There is another way in which support and resistance are related. You might notice sometimes that what was once a resistance level subsequently becomes a resistance level. It seems that the price is reluctant to pass through a particular value... in either direction.

You can see what I mean in *Figure 55 Resistance becomes Support*, where resistance at 70 appears to become support at 70 and where resistance at 75 appears to become support at 75.

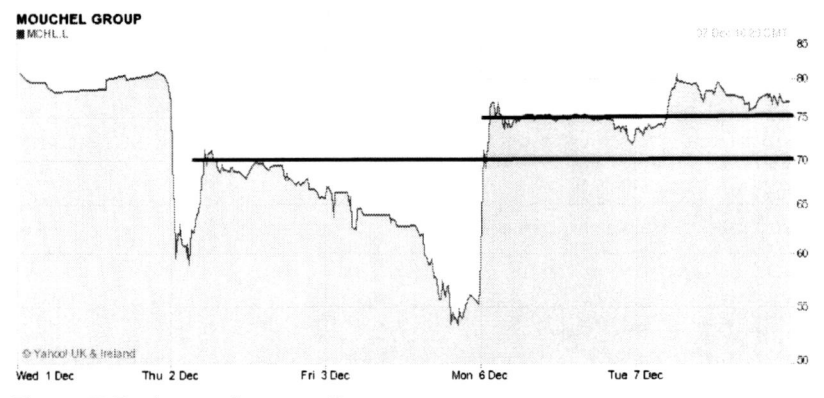

Figure 55 Resistance becomes Support

While I would not generally use this phenomenon to enter a new trade, it may well influence my stop placement on an existing position. When the price ramped up through resistance at 70 on 6 December I might have trailed my stop order to just under that resistance price on the assumption that it would become support – which in this case, it did. When the price rose through apparent resistance at 75 on 7 December, I might have regarded this as the new support level and trailed my stop order accordingly.

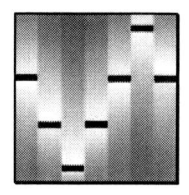

Appendix B – Definitions of "Position Trading"

In the introduction to this book I suggested that while there is some commonality in definitions of the trading style known as position trading, my own personal approach may be subtly different. I present some alternative definitions of position trading below, with my commentary.

From https://securities.standardbank.co.za/ost/nsp/Glossary/glossary.asp?strStartingLetter=P:

"A style of trading characterized by holding open positions for an extended period of time."

I agree with this limited definition providing that the extended period of time is not decided in advance.

From http://ezinearticles.com/?What-is-Position-Trading?&id=412126:

"Position trading is similar to swing trading, but with a longer time horizon. Position traders hold stocks for a time period anywhere from three months to a year."

I agree with this definition as far as it goes, with the proviso that I might hold a position for as little as a day (or even less).

From http://www.free-uk-shares.co.uk/types-of-stock-trading.html:

"Position traders expect to hold on to their stocks for anywhere from 5 days to 3 or 6 months. Position traders are watching for fundamental changes in value of a stock."

I would hold a position for as little as one day (or less), and I am not really interested in stock fundamentals unless / until they are reflected in the price.

From http://daytrading.about.com/od/ptor/g/PositionTrading.htm:

"Chart based position trading really only includes one type of trade: Trend Trading - long term trades that may last anywhere from several days to several weeks, or even longer if the trend continues, with profit targets of several hundreds of ticks."

This definition is probably the closest to position trading as I practice it.

From http://financial-dictionary.thefreedictionary.com/Position+Trading:

"The act or practice of buying and holding. That is, position trading occurs when a trader buys a security and does not sell it until it is at or near maturity. If the security is a stock or otherwise does not have a maturity date, the trader holds it indefinitely."

This is my least favourite definition of position trading from my limited sample of definitions. Although I like to buy and hold, I will not hold indefinitely and unconditionally.

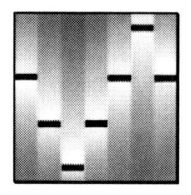

Also by Tony Loton

Tony Loton has written extensively for the Barclays Stockbrokers "Smart Investor" magazine and for the Motley Fool (UK) as well as authoring the following trading and investment books.

Published by Harriman House

***Stop Orders**: A practical guide to using stop orders, for traders and investors*

A stop order is an essential tool used for money management and risk limitation, but for many investors and traders it is not terribly well understood.

This book covers everything you need to know about stop orders and how to make them work for you. Whether you are a trader, an investor, or a spread bettor, you should regard the stop order as essential in helping you lock in your profits and succeed in the markets.

More information and purchase at:

www.lotontech.com/stopordersbook

Tony Loton

Published by LOTON*tech* Limited

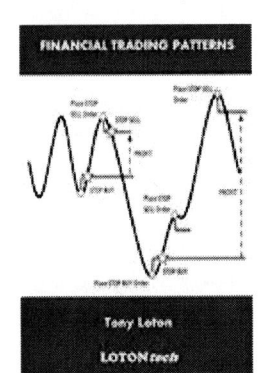

Financial Trading Patterns

This original book covers the various order types offered by your stockbroker, and strategies you can use to incorporate the different orders into your trading. The chapters are laid out in such a way that it is easy to familiarize yourself with each concept, and to understand the pros and cons of the different strategies. Every concept is clearly explained with diagrams and charts, and the success and failure scenarios show how things can go well or badly. The patterns include LIMIT BUY, LIMIT SELL, STOP BUY, STOP SELL, TRAILING STOP BUY, TRAILING STOP SELL, STOP/LIMIT, and STRADDLE. The author rounds off with real-life examples and back-testing results.

DON'T LOSE MONEY! (*in the Stock Markets*)

If your investment falls by 50% you'll need a 100% rise just to get you back where you started. So when speculating in the stock markets, protecting the money you do have is just as important as making some more. This book is for you if you'd like to have a go at beating the system, but don't want to lose your shirt in the process. Topics covered include: index investing, market timing and trend following, stop loss orders, position sizing, and option spreads.

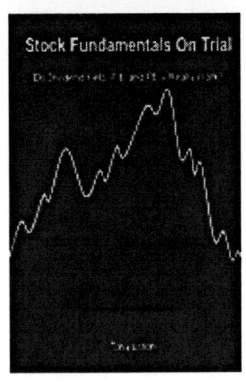

Stock Fundamentals On Trial: *Do Dividend Yield, P/E and PEG Really Work?*

Are high Dividend Yield, low Price / Earnings (P/E) ratio, and low Price / Earnings to Growth (PEG) ratio good indicators of future share price performance -- as conventional wisdom would suggest? Did high yield stocks (the Yield Stars) perform much better than low yield stocks (the Yield Dogs) in recent years? Did low P/E stocks (the P/E Stars) perform much better than high P/E stocks (the P/E Dogs)? What about PEG Stars vs. PEG Dogs? In this book I put company fundamentals on trial, using real historic data and specially annotated charts as evidence. In weighing up the evidence I consider whether the buy-and-hold investor had any advantage over the market timer, and whether stock picking would have been more effective than index investing.

More information and purchase at www.lotontech.com/tradingbooks

Table of Figures

Figure 1 Desire Petroleum Price Gap   34

Figure 2 Stop Order to "Stop a Loss"   38

Figure 3 Stop Order to "Secure a Profit"   38

Figure 4 Trailing Stop Order   39

Figure 5 Prudential 1 March 2010 (tight stop)   43

Figure 6 Rank Group Initial Stop and Trailing Stop   45

Figure 7 Stop Order Danger Zone   48

Figure 8 Pyramiding into National Express   61

Figure 9 Pyramiding into National Express (with Stop Orders)   62

Figure 10 Shanks Group 5 Day Chart   83

Figure 11 Apple 5 Day Price Chart to 18 October 2010   84

Figure 12 Apple 10 Year Price Chart to 18 October 2010   85

Figure 13 Qinetiq 5 Year Price Chart to 2010-10-19   85

Figure 14 Shanks Group 5 Year Chart   87

Figure 15 Bloomsbury 5 Year Chart   89

Figure 16 FTSE 100, 2x Day Trade   92

Figure 17 Prudential 2 March Price Gap Down   97

Figure 18 Shanks Group 9 March Price Gap Down   97

Figure 19 Mouchel Group Price Gap Up   102

Figure 20 FTSE All Share Index 2010-10-20 — 103

Figure 21 Irish Life Daily Chart to mid-November 2010 — 104

Figure 22 Irish Life 5-Minute Chart to 22 November 2010 — 104

Figure 23 The Seven Pillars of Position Trading — 113

Figure 24 Daily Routine — 114

Figure 25 Benefit from Falling Prices — 124

Figure 26 Equity Curve for 3000% in Six Months (2009) — 132

Figure 27 Trading Trail, January - April 2010 — 134

Figure 28 Trading Trail Portfolio at 16 January 2010 — 135

Figure 29 Trading Trail Portfolio at 27 March 2010 — 136

Figure 30 Trading Trail Portfolio (partial) at 24 November 2010 — 137

Figure 31 Trading Trail, the Great Unravel — 137

Figure 32 Trading Trail Draw-Down from Previous Year Winnings — 139

Figure 33 Cumulative Performance to 23 November 2010 — 139

Figure 34 Trading Trail, the Fight-back — 141

Figure 35 Cumulative Performance to 31 December 2010 — 142

Figure 36 FTSE 100 March to September 2009 — 145

Figure 37 Position Trading Cockpit, Live Prices — 150

Figure 38 Position Trading Cockpit, Stop-Out List — 150

Figure 39 Yahoo! Pipes, Latest Prices — 151

Figure 40 Yahoo! Pipes, Stop-Out Price Changes 152

Figure 41 Yahoo! Pipe Example Construction 152

Figure 42 Text Import Wizard, Step 2 or 3 155

Figure 43 Import Data, and External Data Range Properties 156

Figure 44 Calculate % Price Change 156

Figure 45 Conditional Formatting Menu 157

Figure 46 Conditional Formatting Rule 157

Figure 47 Data Validation for Pull-Down List 159

Figure 48 Long and Short Formatting Rule 160

Figure 49 Stop-Out List, Partially Complete 161

Figure 50 Stop-Out List, Complete 162

Figure 51 Google Docs Position Trading Cockpit, Live Prices 163

Figure 52 Google Docs Position Trading Cockpit, Stop-Out List 163

Figure 53 Price Support 180

Figure 54 Price Resistance 181

Figure 55 Resistance becomes Support 182

Index

Average True Range (ATR), 41

averaging down, 31, 57, 58, 59, 60, 61, 62

Beta Adjusted Trailing Stop (BATS), 41

buy and hold, 19, 184

CFD, 42, 43, 44, 48, 66, 73, 94, 108, 123

chart, 45, 80, 87, 91, 92, 100, 117, 134

commodities, 22, 25, 127

covered warrants, 11, 23, 54, 71

currencies, 22, 25, 127

DAX, 30, 36, 73

day trading, 19, 20, 22, 129

diversification, 24, 26, 30, 32, 36, 52, 94, 127, 133

dividend yield, 24, 64, 107, 111

dividends, 19, 22, 24, 44, 45, 63, 64, 65, 73, 107, 108, 109, 110, 111, 128, 129

Don't Lose Money! (in the Stock Markets), 11

Dow Jones, 30, 36, 71

equities, 11, 22, 31, 32, 127

exchange traded funds, 11

fees, 33, 42, 98, 108, 133

Financial Trading Patterns, 11, 15, 186

FTSE 100, 30, 31, 32, 94, 132, 145, 146, 180

fundamental analysis, 15, 79

Gold, 31, 32

indices, 15, 22, 30, 36, 48, 55, 58, 127

interest, 64, 72, 73, 126, 127

Jesse Livermore, 120

Level 2 data, 23

leverage, 16, 21, 22, 24, 26, 33, 71, 72, 76, 79, 146

limit order, 100, 101

margin, 22, 64, 66, 72, 73, 74

market timing, 19, 30, 186

mental stop, 23, 40, 49

money management, 24, 26, 36, 54, 79, 128, 134, 179, 185

Nikkei, 36

P/E, 11, 15, 25, 111, 128, 186

partial close-out, 89, 90, 91, 93

PEG, 11, 15, 25, 111, 128, 186

position sizing, 16, 21, 23, 24, 26, 33, 51, 52, 54, 56, 57, 71, 79, 146, 186 price action, 15, 80, 86, 128, 179

price gap, 34, 55, 82, 97, 100

profit target, 89

pyramid, 61, 63, 65, 66, 67, 93

pyramiding, 16, 21, 26, 31, 33, 56, 57, 60, 61, 69, 70, 79, 81, 90, 91, 93, 95, 108, 123, 146

resistance, 25, 91, 92, 179, 180

reward, 13, 79, 88, 89, 93, 107

risk, 15, 31, 43, 44, 46, 49, 51, 52, 53, 54, 61, 62, 63, 64, 65, 66, 67, 74, 79, 88, 89, 90, 91, 93, 94, 114, 115, 123, 128, 133, 185

S&P 500, 33

Sold List, 80, 81, 95, 96, 101, 117

spread bets, 11, 22, 35, 44, 53, 63, 73, 74, 108, 109, 133

Stock Fundamentals On Trial, 11, 15, 111, 186

stock picking, 24, 26, 79, 80, 105, 186

stocks, 15, 22, 24, 33, 36, 53, 55, 58, 64, 65, 73, 79, 80, 81, 83, 87, 98, 99, 101, 106, 107, 111, 116, 117, 127, 128, 135, 136, 183, 186

stop distance, 40, 44, 45, 48, 49, 54, 116, 179

stop order, 16, 29, 34, 37, 38, 39, 40, 42, 43, 44, 45, 46, 49, 52, 53, 54, 61, 66, 67, 74, 79, 88, 89, 90, 91, 94, 96, 97, 100, 101, 102, 185 stop orders, 15, 16, 21, 23, 24, 26, 31, 33, 37, 39, 40, 41, 45, 46, 48, 49, 52, 53, 54, 60, 61, 62, 65, 66, 71, 72, 89, 91, 94, 99, 115, 118, 120, 123, 134, 146, 185

support, 25, 41, 42, 45, 67, 88, 100, 115, 147, 179

swing trading, 19, 20, 22, 129, 183

Trading Trail, 13, 16, 48, 96, 97, 133, 134, 135, 136, 137, 141, 146

trailing stop order, 39

trend following, 20, 186

Warren Buffett, 19, 29, 41

watch list, 80, 81

whipsaw losses, 40, 46, 96, 97

whipsaw profit, 96, 97

Yahoo! Finance, ii, 83, 115, 116

The End

This is the last printed page of the book. If additional blank pages have been added by the printer, rest assured that you have not missed anything, and you can use the additional pages to make your own notes.

LOTON *tech*

www.lotontech.com

Lightning Source UK Ltd.
Milton Keynes UK
UKOW02f2342011014

239523UK00001B/204/P